On Louise Glück

UNDER DISCUSSION
David Lehman, General Editor
Donald Hall, Founding Editor

Volumes in the Under Discussion series collect reviews and essays about individual poets. The series is concerned with contemporary American and English poets about whom the consensus has not yet been formed and the final vote has not been taken. Titles in the series include:

On Louise Glück

Change What You See

Edited by Joanne Feit Diehl

THE UNIVERSITY OF MICHIGAN PRESS

Ann Arbor

2008 2007 2006 2005   4 3 2 1

A CIP catalog record for this book is available from the British Library.

Library of Congress Cataloging-in-Publication Data

On Louise Glück : change what you see / edited by Joanne Feit Diehl.
        p.   cm. — (Under discussion)
    Includes bibliographical references.
    ISBN 0-472-11479-4 (acid-free paper) — ISBN 0-472-03062-0 (pbk. :
acid-free paper)
    1. Glück, Louise, 1943 — Criticism and interpretation.   2. Women
and literature — United States — History — 20th century.   I. Diehl,
Joanne Feit, 1947–   II. Series.
PS3557.L8Z84 2005
811'.54—dc22

                                                            2004024856

Contents

JOANNE FEIT DIEHL

Introduction

I.

I read to feel addressed: the complement, I suppose, of speaking in order to be heeded.
        —LOUISE GLÜCK, "EDUCATION OF THE POET"

Louise Glück writes poems that bear witness to intimate occasions—subtle, psychological moments captured by the austerity of her diction. Over the years, her style has gone through changes, and indeed one of her virtues is a refusal to stand pat, an insistence that each book be a new point of departure. Yet the initial sense of bearing witness, of testimony, continues to reflect an imagination that confronts experience with bold assurance. While the language of "witness" and "testimony" is frequently associated in our culture with the explicitly political, it nevertheless seems appropriate when characterizing Glück's apolitical work. For the discourse of "testimony" at once implies the immediacy of the speaker's voice and the stance of the observer. Whether she is writing directly of her own experience or projecting feeling into the external world, Glück imparts a clear-sightedness that manifests itself as integrity. Thus her poems embody an apolitical form of testimony that enables Glück to articulate feeling with an impassioned reserve.

I borrow the term "testimony" from Shoshana Felman and Dori Laub's *Testimony: Crises of Witnessing in Literature, Psychoanalysis and History,* which identifies its active, forthright character. "To testify—to *vow to tell,* to *promise* and *produce* one's own speech as material evidence for truth," they write, "is to accomplish a *speech act,* rather than to simply formulate a statement."[1] For Glück, as she states in *Proofs & Theories,* testimony is not the recounting of circumstances but its "transcription."[2] To tell the "truth" is not to recapitulate experience but to reshape events by artistic means. Glück writes, "The source of art is experience, the end product truth, and the artist, surveying the actual, constantly intervenes and manages, lies and deletes, all in the service of truth" (*Proofs & Theories,* 34). By acquiring the illusion of testimony, Glück's poems arrive at a tonal austerity that draws us toward the experience recounted while abjuring the dangers of sentimentality that too frequently mar the work of other, more confessional poets. As Helen Vendler writes in *Part of Nature, Part of Us: Modern American Poets:*

> Glück's cryptic narratives invite our participation: we must, according to the case, fill out the story, substitute ourselves for the fictive personages, invent a scenario from which the speaker can utter her lines, decode the import, "solve" the allegory. Or such is our first impulse. Later, I think, we no longer care. . . . We read the poem, instead, as a truth complete within its own terms, reflecting one of the innumerable configurations into which experience falls. Glück's independent structures, populated by nameless and often ghostly forms engaged in archaic or timeless motions, satisfy without referent. They are far removed from the more circumstantial poetry written by women poets in the last ten years, but they remain poems chiefly about childhood, family life, love, and motherhood. In their obliquity and reserve, they offer an alternative to first-person "confession," while remaining indisputably personal.[3]

In the early poems, the reader engages in the act of empathic witnessing most strongly in those moments when the poet embraces the clarity of direct statement, those moments when language borders on silence, when thought cannot be more sparely articulated. The force of these moments achieves the authority of an oracular power, which has become one of the hallmarks of Glück's style. The tone of dispassion so frequently heard in the poems contributes to this achievement by invoking the withheld power of restraint. The opening of "The Drowned Children," in *Descending Figure,* startles with this power:[4]

> You see, they have no judgment.
> So it is natural that they should drown,
> first the ice taking them in
> and then, all winter, their wool scarves
> floating behind them as they sink
> until at last they are quiet.
> And the pond lifts them in its manifold dark arms.

The shock of the accidental has been replaced by the more astonishing tone of the matter-of-fact. The lines are weighted with an inevitability that stems from the unquestioning assurance of the opening statement followed by a dispassionate recounting of the fully imagined yet strangely disembodied children and concluding with the pond's plaintive personification as it "lifts them in its manifold dark arms." In this passage, Glück conveys through a process of withholding a tamping down of emotion which she releases only in the synecdochic figure of the pond's strangely maternal arms. Here as elsewhere restraint defers emotion, creating the uncanny effect of drawing us into the poem while insisting upon the opacity of experience.

In "Parodos," the opening poem of *Ararat* (1990), the speaker states the ideal of testimony as her fate:

> I'll tell you
> what I meant to be—
> a device that listened . . .
> Not inert: still.
> A piece of wood. A stone.
> . . . .
> I was born to a vocation:
> to bear witness
> to the great mysteries.
> Now that I've seen both
> birth and death, I know
> to the dark nature these
> are proofs, not
> mysteries—

Glück achieves her austere narrative voice by combining an apparently objective stance with a declarative mode that simultaneously invites us in even as it repels intimacy. This stark probity of style accentuates the power of the witness. Yet elsewhere, the very characteristics that inform this authoritative, testamentary style are called into question. In "The Untrustworthy Speaker," the "I" questions the trustworthiness of her voice, urging us not to "listen" to her. Having "learned to hear like a psychiatrist," the speaker distrusts her capacity to remain objective, doubting her ability to witness with accuracy. She acknowledges her rhetorical ruse of invisibility:

In my own mind, I'm invisible: that's why I'm dangerous.
People like me, who seem selfless,
we're the cripples, the liars;
we're the ones who should be factored out
in the interest of truth.

Only in the role of the silent observer does the speaker witness the "truth":

When I'm quiet, that's when the truth emerges.
A clear sky, the clouds like white fibers.
Underneath, a little gray house, the azaleas
red and bright pink.

To understand what inhabits this house, the speaker directs the auditor "to close yourself / to the older daughter, block her out: / when a living thing is hurt like that, / in its deepest workings, / all function is altered":

That's why I'm not to be trusted.
Because a wound to the heart
is also a wound to the mind.

And yet, despite this warning, the wounded speaker keeps bearing witness, assessing the burdens of her subjectivity. "Brown Circle," from *Ararat,* describes the negative power of the wounded self that continues to speak. Structured as an interrogation, the poem presents a dialogue between the speaker and the speaker's mother, who "wants to know / why, if I hate / family so much, / I went ahead and / had one." This question introduces reflections on the nature of the speaker's relation to her son, for the poem's real subject is how the speaker loves him:

I don't love my son
the way I meant to love him.
I thought I'd be
the lover of orchids who finds
red trillium growing
in the pine shade, and doesn't
touch it, doesn't need
to possess it. What I am

is the scientist,
who comes to that flower
with a magnifying glass
and doesn't leave, though
the sun burns a brown
circle of grass around
the flower. Which is
more or less the way
my mother loved me.

I must learn
to forgive my mother,
now that I'm helpless
to spare my son.

The requisite forgiveness of her mother comes only by recognizing the repetition that stains her relation to her son. Glück here associates damage with care, gesturing toward the dangers of intimacy, the risks of an obsessive, maternal empathy.

Such obsessive watchfulness is matched by a will to silence as physical gestures acquire the expressive force of speech. In "Terminal Resemblance," Glück marks the final meeting of father and daughter with a gesture:

When I saw my father for the last time, we both did the same
    thing.
. . . .
We said goodbye in the usual way,
no embrace, nothing dramatic.
When the taxi came, my parents watched from the front
    door,
arm in arm, my mother blowing kisses as she always does,
because it frightens her when a hand isn't being used.
But for a change, my father didn't just stand there.
This time, he waved.

That's what I did, at the door to the taxi.
Like him, waved to disguise my hand's trembling.

Here, however, gesture does not simply convey emotion; it disguises it. Yet we, her readers, are let in on the secret that the speaker will not otherwise disclose. This interplay of gesture and speech reduces explanation to a minimum contained in another physical move-ment, her "hand's trembling." Feeling invests itself in gesture, and the retrospective recounting of that disguising wave and what it hides bears witness to the emotion that informs it.

Teleology haunts other poems as well, and it is this "sense of an ending" that infuses Glück's poems with their retrospective power. As the speaker of "Celestial Music" remarks, "The love of form is a love of endings." In "Mirror Image," the speaker, with an inevitable-seeming simplicity, comments on her father's (and her own) obses-sion with death:

> Tonight I saw myself in the dark window as
> the image of my father, whose life
> was spent like this,
> thinking of death, to the exclusion
> of other sensual matters,
> so in the end that life
> was easy to give up, since
> it contained nothing: even
> my mother's voice couldn't make him
> change or turn back
> as he believed
> that once you can't love another human being
> you have no place in the world.

The taut lines swiftly draw the reader's eyes to the closing insight, the enjambments contributing to the sound of the unflinching voice, a voice that speaks with the power of the witness. Observa-tion will brook no detour into the comforts of artificial solace.

No subject is too small or too insignificant to bear meaning for Glück. In "Children Coming Home from School," the fact that her sister rides in a stroller becomes the occasion for a haunting sense of homelessness that possesses the older daughter as she watches her mother's and sibling's approach. Of her sister riding in the stroller, the speaker observes:

> She didn't see we were both in false positions.
> She wanted freedom. Whereas I continued, in pathetic ways,
> to covet the stroller. Meaning
> all my life.

And, in that sense, it was lost on me: all the waiting, all my
    mother's
effort to restrain my sister, all the calling, the waving,
since, in that sense, I had no home any longer.

Never, perhaps, has a stroller played such an existential role in a
poem. And it is just this capacity to render the pathos in the quotidian that marks Glück as a Wordsworthian poet. Surely she is heir
to the Romantic sensibility, although the astringency of the poems
speaks to a singularity of voice that she shares with Emily Dickinson. The final poem of *Ararat,* "First Memory," speaks to her
wounded self, offering a prophetic insight in the form of an echo
from the past:

> Long ago, I was wounded. I lived
> to revenge myself
> against my father, not
> for what he was—
> for what I was: from the beginning of time,
> in childhood, I thought
> that pain meant
> I was not loved.
> It meant I loved.

In this assumption of responsibility, the speaker utters the volume's
closing words and returns us to its beginnings, to the voice of
"*Parodos,*" and to its first line, "Long ago, I was wounded." Recalling what has transpired from that first articulation of a wounded
self to the final recollection of wounding, the self-accusing poetic
"I" testifies to the deprivations and hardships of the familial as it simultaneously reflects a sensibility drawn toward the telos of existence, the quotidian imbued with the symbolic power of myth.
Characteristically, Glück uses myth in a compensatory way, restoring to mythological characters the immediacy of human emotion
while drawing on the resonance of the ancient to invest the contemporary with the cumulative weight of epic associations.

It is just this fusion of the mythic and the quotidian that is mag-
isterially articulated in *Meadowlands* (1996). If her preceding volume,
The Wild Iris (1992), presents a polyphony of voices—god, human
being, the garden—the prevailing tone of that work is fairly constant, a version of the plangent, pastoral sublime. But in *Meadowlands*

the tonal scope is much broader, ranging from the lyrical to the outrageously comic. Evocations of the epic story of Penelope and Odysseus intermix with poems of a contemporary, divorcing couple, and this juxtaposition lends a new valence to Glück's earlier austerity while the poems maintain a very real tie to that originally austere voice. Here, the two voices that have emerged in her earlier work, the demotic voice of our contemporary and the mythic voice that inhabits the distanced yet intimate sphere of the imagination, merge. The ancient past and the demotic present come together, borrowing from each other's worlds of feeling. Interspersed among these poems are conversations conducted by a couple on the verge of separation. Forceful as well as funny, these poems enact the tensions which the surrounding poems imply. Given the complications of aesthetic merger and the vexing politics of humor, the question arises how best to address the reader, how to configure the relation between audience and text to render these poems open to interpretation. To explore this relation in *Meadowlands,* it is first necessary to observe the twining of voices that occurs during the course of individual poems so that the present and the past constitute an ahistorical continuum of consciousness. From the very first poem of the volume, "Penelope's Song," with its allusion to Maria Callas, we realize that we are in a realm where ordinary chronologies have no hold. Moving back and forth through time, later poems braid past and present, as in "Quiet Evening":

You take my hand; then we're alone
in the life-threatening forest. Almost immediately

we're in a house; Noah's
grown and moved away; the clematis after ten years
suddenly flowers white.

More than anything in the world
I love these evenings when we're together,
the quiet evenings in summer, the sky still light at this hour.

So Penelope took the hand of Odysseus,
not to hold him back but to impress
this peace on his memory:

from this point on, the silence through which you move
is my voice pursuing you.

This conjunction of the contemporary and the ancient is first introduced by the mystery of place in the poem's opening:

> You take my hand; then we're alone
> in the life-threatening forest. Almost immediately
>
> we're in a house. . . .

The inexplicable, sudden change of place, from forest to house, reminds us of the world of dream, where such abrupt shifts effortlessly occur. Thematically, too, the oneiric context is appropriate, as the poem revolves around separation and homecoming, departure and return. The contemporary impinges upon the antique in ways that interweave aspects of mythic consciousness into current crisis. By fusing these two realms, Glück creates for her readers a privileged position, as we, like the author, move interpretively among registers of psychic experience. We are guided by a narrative voice that moves between these registers with consummate ease, intermingling the Odyssean story of return with the contemporary breakup of a marriage. The tone shifts abruptly from the relative lyricism of "Penelope's Song," "Cana," and "Quiet Evening" to the biting humor of "Ceremony." This poem and others like it, "Rainy Morning," "Anniversary," and "Meadowlands I," combine the *frisson* of wit with an underlying bitterness. Instances of humor laced with pain, these poems contribute to the unfolding dynamic of the contemporary lovers' relationship. Glück complicates these poems' wry tone with the sardonic asides of "Telemachus' Detachment":

> When I was a child looking
> at my parents' lives, you know
> what I thought? I thought
> heartbreaking. Now I think
> heartbreaking, but also
> insane. Also
> very funny.

Detachment is not, however, reserved for Telemachus; it also enters into the narrative voice's description of Odyssean events, as in "Parable of the Hostages":

The Greeks are sitting on the beach
wondering what to do when the war ends. No one
wants to go home, back
to that bony island; everyone wants a little more
of what there is in Troy, more
life on the edge, that sense of every day as being
packed with surprises. . .
. . . what if war
is just a male version of dressing up,
a game devised to avoid
profound spiritual questions?

A similar ironic detachment marks Circe's speech, in "Circe's Power":

> My friend,
> every sorceress is
> a pragmatist at heart; nobody
> sees essence who can't
> face limitation. If I wanted only to hold you
>
> I could hold you prisoner.

In these lines, wit jolts passion to create a *realpolitik* of desire. Such moments mark Glück's version of the Sublime, wherein the brevity of aphorism is infused with the plangency of irrecoverable loss. Indeed, loss shadows all the poems of *Meadowlands,* a loss made inevitable by the passage of time and the human events of history. In "Nostos," the speaker concludes, "We look at the world once, in childhood. / The rest is memory."

Thematically, what counters this intertwining narrative of disillusionment and always-potential loss is the impulse to write poems. While the projected "other" imagines that the speaker desires him to return to her, the "I" wishes for something altogether different, as in "The Wish":

> Remember that time you made the wish?
>
> I make a lot of wishes.
>
> The time I lied to you
> about the butterfly. I always wondered
> what you wished for.

What do you think I wished?

I don't know. That I'd come back,
that we'd somehow be together in the end.

I wished for what I always wish for.
I wished for another poem.

Passionate feelings inform ambition's wish; Glück, through her speaker, here proclaims the reassertion of desire in her quest for art. Reading *Meadowlands,* we discover that the poems form a continuum wherein the shifting tonal registers contribute to a sustained sequence that intertwines diverse feelings held together by motifs of return and loss. The reader of these poems becomes, therefore, the one who is called upon to bear witness, the one who overhears, the one who is positioned to create a unified vision from disparate experiences.

If, in her two recent volumes *Vita Nova* (1999) and *The Seven Ages* (2001), Glück introduces a more balanced, accepting view of the world, the poems also resume the stance of the witness. Speaking in the voices of the contemporary poet and of ancient, mythic personae, these poems extend the paradigms of Glück's earlier work. Along with newly supple modulations in voice and surprising shifts in the character of Glück's experiences, the role of the witness remains central to her poems. Writing of the strong poets of the past, Glück asserts:

> Substantial contributions to our collective inheritance were made by poets whose poems seemed blazingly personal, as though the poets had performed autopsies on their own living tissue. The presence of the speaker in these poems was overwhelming; the poems read as testaments, as records of the life. Art was redefined, all its ingenuities washed away. (*Proofs & Theories,* 35)

Glück takes up this "collective inheritance" and makes it her own as she reinvents the "blazingly personal" testimony that speaks with uncompromised integrity of the events that summon most clearly the powers of her poetic imagination.

In what follows, I briefly summarize this volume's critical chapters, as these, too, in different ways, witness aspects of Glück's aesthetics of poetic voice.

II.

Let Change Transfuse All Other Traits
—EMILY DICKINSON, POEM 1731 (F.)

In this volume's opening statement, Frank Bidart reminds us that, although others speak of Glück in the highest possible terms, she herself has most often turned her eye to self-critique. Bidart goes on to note that "a little collection could be made of the negative things that Glück has said about herself. This is not an attempt to charm; it is part of the poems' air of astringency, of applying the same disabused intelligence to the self that the self applies to the world." Bidart attributes the "*accent of fatality* characteristic of her lines" to her seeing "'one thing at a time' so profoundly that common seeing by comparison shrivels." Taking Glück's *The Wild Iris* as his exemplary text, Bidart points out the volume's "startling structure," which Glück balances with the "protean, prodigal variety of Glück's 'fierce seeing of only one thing at a time.'" Bidart goes on to assess Glück's volumes, noting their continuities and differences. Drawing attention to her focus on form, and her "constantly fresh and unexpected way of *stationing* the self," Bidart illustrates the growth of this act of stationing from volume to volume. Bidart closes by recommending to us the experience he has just had: "over the course of two weeks read Louise Glück's nine books of poetry, in the order in which she published them." Bidart's appreciation of Glück's poems introduces thematic concerns that run through the book as a whole: the distinct slant (as Dickinson might say) of her vision, her "mastery" of structure, and the capacity for intimacy freed from the circumstantial.

Wayne Koestenbaum, in his contribution, originally the introduction to a poetry reading by Glück on February 4, 2002, at the 92nd Street Y, holds Glück in equally high esteem. For him her work is crucial, the contemporary voice that makes the life of the imagination in our time possible. "Without her work," Koestenbaum states, "I cannot imagine the world." For Koestenbaum Glück's poems transcend their genre, serving as "pedagogy, creed, philosophy." He goes on to characterize Glück's poetry as "concise, precise, hard, reticent, unsentimental, spare." He speaks of the poems as a "nervy antidote" to what "Tennessee Williams called 'mendacity.'" The source of Koestenbaum's admiration for Glück's poems is their "sting." He places her work in the context of her "predecessors in the pursuit of the minimalist ecstatic (Sappho, Dickinson, Cavafy, Oppen, Éluard, Ponge)" and concludes his remarks by expressing his admiration for the essential quality of Glück's accomplishment, the writing of works that are "purely 'poem,'" the creation of a poetry that speaks both to our silences and to our speech.

Linda Gregerson returns to Glück's forebears as well, singling out the major tradition of lyric poetry in English, and within this context addressing Glück's sixth book (*The Wild Iris*) and her seventh (*Meadowlands*) to illuminate a change from the earlier to the later work: a "deepening so remarkable that it amounts to a new departure." Gregerson introduces this discussion by asserting the centrality of Glück for contemporary poetry and poetics, her production of work that is "justly admired and justly influential." These volumes, Gregerson writes, are "two poles of a single project" that come late in the life of the lyric tradition. Interested initially in the form of *The Wild Iris,* Gregerson notes that it is "an interwoven series of dramatic monologues." Gregerson traces the manifestations of the three voices of *The Wild Iris:* "(1) those spoken by a human persona to God, or to that which holds the place of God; (2) those spoken by the botanical inhabitants of the garden cultivated by the human persona; and (3) those spoken by divinity." Despite the book's complexity and mordant ironies, Gregerson reminds us, there is the "troubling possibility, indeed, the certain knowledge, that its analogies are false or partial." She introduces in this regard the Renaissance process of "accommodation": "Because we are weak, because we cannot behold divinity face to face, God 'accommodates' himself to our limits, agreeing to be known by elements available to human sense. These measures, however, are imperfect and interim." In another way, too, *The Wild Iris* resembles its forebears, Gregerson asserts, as "the garden is a sign because it is redolent with absence": "The sharers in the garden come to know themselves by knowing that something is missing; their very failure to sustain one another is part of the message." Reading *The Wild Iris* within this lyric tradition, Gregerson reminds us that the "triangular manipulation of presence" (the dominant structure of the poem sequence) "is as old as the lyric itself." Yet such triangulation remains uncertain, for, as in the lyric throughout history, what gives the work "urgency" is the "spectral possibility . . . not that the beloved isn't listening, but that the beloved doesn't exist." When, however, the fiction of dialogue is maintained, Gregerson notes, Glück achieves a "marvelous mobility of tone" more developed in this volume than in previous ones.

These voices speak in the language of domestic irony, and it is, according to Gregerson, the deployment of the familial that marks the distinctive quality of Glück's tone. But the exchange of speech, the presence of an auditor, may be only an illusion, for "in *The Wild Iris* as in its dominant line of lyric forebears, unrequited longing is the constitutive feature of consciousness."

Glück, according to Gregerson, approaches both volumes through the lens of a "structural insight: the deployment of inherited patterns . . . on a book-length scale." These patterns include the "domestic quarrel," wherein the "soul-destroying can be transmuted to the spirit-reviving." What carries out this transformation is Glück's mastery of the "structure of domestic dialogue." This dialogue provides the power for the poems not only of *The Wild Iris* but of *Meadowlands* as well. What constitutes Glück's "structural insight," in Gregerson's words, what is a "part of their wit," is their tracing of great epic themes and their positing of "conversation in a fertile world: my part, yours, the whole making more than the sum of its parts."

The question of reliability, of trustworthiness of voice, is the subject of Bonnie Costello's chapter. After succinctly summing up the limitations of Glück's earlier narrators, Costello introduces the strengths of Glück's narrators in her recently published poems, presenting the crucial differences that account for such apparent trustworthiness. Self-awareness, which can be a form of self-regard, moves throughout *Meadowlands,* as illustrated by Costello when she cites "Penelope's Song," which, she argues, "is alert to motive and wary of histrionics, without retreating into a bland objectivity." The balance in these poems between "subjectivity" and "scrutiny" creates, according to Costello, the voice of the "trustworthy" narrator in whom we can believe. Costello is careful to distinguish between damaging self-regard and accurate soul see(k)ing. She writes of both *The Wild Iris* and *Meadowlands* as participating in "lyric's great task, yet distinguish[ing] [this task] from a narcissism that refuses to delimit the self." Costello draws our attention to the three strategies of "American Narcissism" that "discourage narcissistic entrapment." In a list of qualities that could be associated with Marianne Moore as well as with Glück, Costello notes the three "imaginative maneuvers" as "modesty, humor, and detachment." What is new specifically in *Meadowlands* is that in this volume when Glück draws upon archetypal stories she emphasizes not "psychological depth or metaphysical reflection" but "dramatic possibility."

Part of the tonal balance of *Meadowlands,* Costello reminds us, is due to humor, yet humor that does not relinquish the voice's more serious tone. Identifying what is new in this humor within the tradition of tragicomic poets, Costello remarks: "This is her funniest volume, yet the humor is not trivializing; the somber music retains its claim on the emotions. *Meadowlands* offers a new kind of tragicomedy, less grotesque than Eliot's, less black than Beckett's, more constructive than Berryman's." In her discussion of the techniques Glück practices to maintain a balanced yet subjectively inflected voice, Costello draws special attention to the parable, which, with its objectivity and "abstract and impersonal" tone, establishes distance between speaker and experience. Perhaps most telling is Costello's insight that "parables clarify while asserting the underlying mystery in the way things are; hence they often present paradoxes and find truth in enigma." Fables also serve a defamiliarizing purpose and contribute to the poems' "humor."

Alan Williamson also homes in on the question of voice in *Meadowlands* and clarifies what we hear. "The divorce poems," Williamson argues in his chapter, are moving not only because they create a dialogue that captures, "so perfectly, the unkindnesses only people who know each other intimately are capable of," but also because they "feel like a dialogue between the two forces that have warred in Glück's poetry from early on." Contextualizing *Meadowlands* in the shifting tone of the later poems, Williamson notes how slow critics have been to acknowledge Glück as a comic poet. He astutely observes that such a shift need not seem so surprising since "one cannot remain forever in the posture of disappointment or protest against 'vitality.' To stand outside everyone else's modes of hope and comfort, yet express more than childlike stubbornness, is to become a satirist: Swift's stance, not Shelley's." Before he approaches *Meadowlands,* Williamson invokes my concept of American women poets' relation to what I have called the "Counter-Sublime." Reminding us that Glück belongs to a different poetic generation than Dickinson, Moore, Bishop, or Plath, he puts my theory of poetic conflict to the test in reading Glück's work. Elsewhere I have argued that because of gender, women experience the Sublime differently, as a conflict between a defensive subject and "an essential adversary." Because Glück's "distrust of the 'nature of things' is still gendered, still in some way a refusal of an invasive male presence, as well as of easy male affirmations," Williamson reads her as the most recent woman poet in the genealogy I have posited. Williamson concludes this discussion by asserting that "Glück's way of manifesting splendor, emotional and linguistic, in the act of defending against it is the very essence of the Counter-Sublime."

Recognizing in Glück the verbal form of depressive realism, "the notion . . . that some depressed people prove especially good at predicting what they and others will do, because their divorce from their own hopes makes them able to see, and willing to describe, facts and emotions the rest of us block or deny," Stephen Burt understands this tendency as a key to Glück's work. And, he continues, "coming to love a Glück poem means coming to empathize with the bitter self-consciousness her skeletal arrangements reflect." Elaborating on and historicizing this theory, Burt suggests that Glück's best work from the 1970s and 1980s "had precisely this effect, surprising us with the persistent disjunction between its common words and its exceptional states of feeling." This particular deployment of diction, Glück's rejection of the circumstantial among other effects, means that "Glück's depressive style makes other kinds of aesthetic choices (chiefly structural and grammatical) bear exceptional weight." Burt asserts that her poems "struggle . . . against an unusually strong impetus toward closure . . . [that] comes in part from the ways they seem always ready to stop."

Burt argues that this method of conclusion, the gesture of repudiation, operates not only within a single poem, but from volume to volume. Burt remarks, "Glück's drive to repudiate, revise and draw new conclusions operates not only within her poems, but from one book to the next." "Every one of her books of poetry," Burt asserts, quoting Glück, "'has culminated in a conscious diagnostic act, a swearing-off.'" It is part of Burt's project to see "how *Meadowlands* responds to Glück's earlier work" and to show what "rhythmic, grammatical, and structural choices still propel her poems, and still distinguish them from one another." A close technical reading of poems from *Meadowlands* leads to further valuable insights, including Burt's assertion that "where other poets change moods by changing images or adjectives, Glück alters her pace." Here, at the chapter's close, Burt, like Costello, considers a parable from *Meadowlands,* "Parable of the Gift," to conclude that "her poems of multiple endings, pressing on past the points where they might have stopped, embody the depressive realist's unasked-for skill at seeing past illusions, seeing through the conclusions with which others might have been happy." Such seeing, Burt notes, is what embodies her stance as a "depressive realist." He is "fascinated" by her poems because "she makes anhedonia interesting."

Paul Breslin, on the other hand, brings a greater degree of skepticism to Glück's poetry. Casting her work in a Blakean frame, Breslin identifies Glück with the "Devouring" portion in *The Marriage of Heaven and Hell*. Reading her work chronologically, Breslin moves quickly to *The House on Marshland* (1975), with its attainment of "a quiet, laconic voice so calm, given the implied intensity of what it evokes, as to seem numb, traumatized." It is, however, with her third book, *Descending Figure* (1980), that Breslin recognizes an essential voice, "a poet [he] must read." Taking the controversial poem "The Drowned Children" as his prime example, Breslin shows how the seductive and beautiful icy waters beneath which the children drown have more agency than the children's parents. Remarking upon Glück's tone of "mute astonishment at the fragility of life," Breslin believes that the deadened "affect" of this poem is a sign of terror, not indifference.

Observing that "the social texture of Glück's poetry is thinner than that of any other poet who impresses [him] so much," Breslin asserts that the poems of the past twenty years engage gender politics, focusing on "Glück's early struggles with anorexia nervosa." Citing Ludwig Binswanger's "The Case of Ellen West," Breslin notes that, finishing this case history, he had an "overwhelming sense of having been shown an interiority that would have been unimaginable to [him] without Binswanger's mediation." Breslin continues: "And this is akin to what I derive from Glück's poems, except that here the mediation has been achieved by the same person who has endured the experience, and that in itself is a significant achievement." Writing on the deployment of myth in Glück's poems, particularly the character Telemachus in the "Odyssey" poems in *Meadowlands,* Breslin astutely observes that Telemachus, "in a defiant assertion of his autonomy, . . . disavows emotions that, against his will, his own utterance helplessly reveals."

For the remainder of his chapter, Breslin concentrates on the two books he likes best: *Ararat* and *The Wild Iris*. These volumes he perceives as marking the "polarities of [Glück's] imagination." *The Wild Iris,* according to Breslin, "translates the personal into natural metaphors," whereas *Ararat* is the "most unabashedly autobiographical of her books since *Firstborn,* but with a technical mastery and restraint gained in the twenty-two years between." The whole of the sequence of flower poems Breslin reads as an analogy that underpins the sequence: "god is to the creation as gardener is to flowers, and as poet is to poem." According to Breslin, the book ends on "an affirmative note" because it "so fully acknowledges the pressure of mortality"; the speaker's "suffering, her abandonment . . . has been visited on her in order to bring forth the splendor of eternity, as one buries a bulb in order to bring forth a flower." Given this interpretation, Breslin selects *The Wild Iris* as the "most capacious and generous volume of her poems to date," a book that "allows the Prolific to answer the Devouring."

Rather than focus on the sweep of Glück's career, Sandra M. Gilbert, in her chapter, directs her attention to *Vita Nova*. Early in her discussion, Gilbert reminds us that, like some of Glück's earlier books, *Vita Nova* has the "weighty austerity of myth or, perhaps more accurately, the statuary of myth"—archaic figures of, say, "Ulysses, Penelope, Aeneas, Eurydice, Dido, Orpheus." Yet this is not always the case, and elsewhere, according to Gilbert, Glück's poems "seem torn from a small far suffering place that is beyond or behind the stony accretions of mythic sculpture." In a larger context, Gilbert asserts that "Glück's main concern as an artist has always been with the great questions myth and its statuary seek to ask (and answer)." Gilbert marks a shift between the first "Vita Nova" of the volume and the last poem of the sequence of the same title, a poem that connotes Glück's ambivalence toward the healing possibilities of rebirth: "By the time Glück rewrites her opening 'Vita Nova' as the volume's concluding poem," writes Gilbert, "even the tenderest messages of death have been elided by the salutary toughness of a very funny (and plainly therapeutic) sendup of therapy and its discontents." Interpreting Glück's quest for self-recognition and a new life, Gilbert notes the difficulties of such a process. Alluding briefly to specific poems, Gilbert introduces the poignant and affirmative "Nest," with its hope for renewal. Thus Gilbert acknowledges the complexity of Glück's renewal and the ambivalent tones in which she describes this process of rebirth.

Like Gilbert, James Longenbach recognizes the new rising from the old in Glück's poetry. Centering his discussion on *Vita Nova*, Longenbach describes the changes that occur between Glück's earlier sequences and this book. Asserting that "change is Louise Glück's highest value," Longenbach notes that the poems of *Vita Nova* do not retreat "to an extreme of diction or sensibility"; rather, these later poems "ultimately feel at home in a fluctuating middle ground that is not a compromise between extremes." Change must affect how we imagine the past as well as our visions for the future. Longenbach explains, "In *Vita Nova* the act of imagining the future is contingent upon the act of reimagining–rather than rejecting—the past." Instead of situating this book in its thematics–the "death of love" and the "rebirth of vocation"—Longenbach asserts that *Vita Nova*'s real drama is the "unfolding dialogue between 'material' and 'form,' the way in which past experience is refigured in the language of poetry." Yet the change that is the hallmark of Glück's poetic trajectory is, in *Vita Nova,* not a rejection, but an acceptance that "truly meaningful change must inevitably be partial change—complicit, incomplete": "Glück learns to live within repetition, and the result is, paradoxically, something really new: a reconsideration of the structure and function of lyric poetry."

Longenbach switches back to an overview of Glück's poems to emphasize what he considers to be their "presiding technical problem"—"the placement of the speaker relative to the material." He leads us through the sequence of Glück's books to reveal his understanding of how this placement shifts. Comparing *Vita Nova* to *Meadowlands,* Longenbach writes, "If *Meadowlands* exteriorizes as dialogue the conflicts lyric poems more often interiorize as ambiguity, *Vita Nova* is uttered by a single speaker who contains within herself a variety of overlapping, eccentric positions." According to Longenbach, the subject of *Vita Nova* is less that of the "breakup of a marriage" than of the "poet's subsequent attempt to reorder her experience." Formulating a thought that recalls that of Elizabeth Bishop in "Northhaven," her elegy for Robert Lowell—"Repeat, repeat, repeat / Revise, revise, revise"—Glück understands in *Vita Nova* that "to exist in time is necessarily to exist in repetition; to exist successfully in time is to recognize that what is returned to us—hope or despair—repeats the past with a difference." Longenbach argues that the "real achievement" of *Vita Nova* lies not in poems that "carry their weight in their final lines," but in a "new kind of lyric structure, one that embodies a love of the middle rather than a 'love of endings.'" For Longenbach, "Glück's embracing of repetition seems . . . the crucial development in *Vita Nova:* the structure of the poems, their attitude toward change, and their relationship to Glück's earlier work all depend on it."

In my chapter, I suggest, like Longenbach, that this book is not only the record of the poet's journey but also a rendering of how her poetry changes in light of it. In *Vita Nova,* I discern a renewed openness to the benign possibilities of the world. In "Aubade," we awaken to the "pleasures of the material world: to color, texture, and change." Yet such openness to life's plenitude does not erase this and other poems' "desire to render extreme affective states and to attend to Glück's familiar dramas of suffering, which inform an only partial turn from grief." I go on to observe that several poems ("The Queen of Carthage," "The Burning Heart," "Eurydice," and "Relic") voice the "powerful exigencies that arise as a woman contemplates her fate." In the first poem, Dido "makes of destiny a willed and conscious choice. What further dignifies her action is her closing reinterpretation of fate itself." In fact, both this poem and "Eurydice" seize upon the moment when fate traditionally speaks: "By restoring language and thereby the power of choice to Dido and Eurydice, these poems expand the expressive possibilities of writing as a survivor and thereby asserting agency over experience." In my discussion of other poems, as well, I conclude that the new openness to experience, what I call an "embrace of the material world," is but one side of an "aesthetic dichotomy" operating in *Vita Nova*. Hence it goes without saying that such an operative dichotomy raises "antithetical possibilities for interpretation." This form, I continue, allows for an interesting kind of freedom; for, while the structure of the interlocutory serves to shape the narrative response, that response nevertheless is free to reassign emphases and define meaning to construct its own story. Glück's process of inquiry "alters the fundamental character of self-disclosure, substituting for the declamatory a more nuanced, interactive cadence." *Vita Nova* presents an experiential dichotomy as the impulse to embrace the material world offset by inflections of doubt. Evaluating *Vita Nova* in relation to Glück's earlier works, I find a convergence of hitherto oppositional voices, especially the voices of mythic women who, in this volume, seize for themselves the moment of fate and convert it into a decisive moment of agency. The turn to the world is accompanied by the reassertion of Glück's power as female descendant of these voices and foremost as poet.

Recounting his first conversation with Glück and remarking upon her choice of the word "imminent" to describe the weather, Stephen Yenser draws a brief comparison between Emily Dickinson's diction and Glück's. Yenser broadens his comments to include a mutual convergence of sensibilities: "no one else of her approximate age reminds me as often of Dickinson as the earlier Glück." For Yenser, Glück's early poems bespeak a kind of minimalist economy that allows her simultaneously to be "absent and present," "laconic and eloquent," "chary and rich," "astringent and energetic." Commenting specifically on *Vita Nova,* Yenser asserts that it sometimes seems "committed to a certain austerity and minimalism." He claims that this volume contains Glück's swearing off, her turn against her earlier style. Yenser remarks: "*Vita Nova* purports to be the beginning of a new mode—or at least the end of the old one. Further, the book often indicts the poet's own earlier manner." Yenser, in one of a number of close readings, finds in the opening poem of the volume, "Vita Nova," "at least two tones [that] fade into each other . . . as smoothly as the enjambed lines override the syntactical units, and the balance struck is tipped word by word in the last line in the direction of melancholic irony." He understands "Descent to the Valley" as containing lines that form "a powerful critique of Glück's earlier work." But the project of resolving individual poems' ambiguities in *Vita Nova* is one in which Yenser places no confidence. Instead he understands the collection as a cohesive project, a "constellation" if not a sequence, that springs from opposing forces or impulses, which Glück names or alludes to repeatedly. Extending that project, Yenser provides a provisional chart of dichotomies that, despite his own skepticism, enables readers to acknowledge the *agon* between oppositional terms. Writing of Glück's subsequent volume, *The Seven Ages,* Yenser states that these "recent poems testify to a sense of acceptance hitherto rare in Glück's work." According to Yenser, in "Birthday" she "now discovers felicity when she recognizes change." In a comparison between the late Yeats and T. S. Eliot on the one hand and Glück on the other, Yenser comments upon the contrast he sees between the older poets and Glück: specifically he notes the resemblance between Glück's "The Traveler" and "Little Gidding." Yet he witnesses, too, the "dangers in conjuring such a 'dead master' or rival 'predecessor' as Eliot." Central to the difference between Eliot and Glück are tone and a *jouissance* that Yenser finds present at times in Eliot but absent in the later poet's work. But his larger "point is that, against her own steely resistance, the originally anxious, absolutist, minimalist Louise Glück has opened her poems up." Yenser culminates his discussion of the achievement that *Vita Nova* and *The Seven Ages* represent by asserting that "the poems in the last two volumes move—and, to my mind, they are therefore the more moving."

If, as the chapters in this volume assert, Glück has extended her range, reshaping our relationship to the poems so that we participate more fully in the creation of meaning, and if the more recent work gestures toward a greater openness to life, we must nevertheless acknowledge the continuity between her earliest poems and her most recent. The evolution of Glück's experimentation with the powers of voice points to the expansiveness of an aural imagination that will, no doubt, persist to modulate into still other, yet-to-be-heard poetic forms. Each of the writers in this volume addresses the subject of change and the role it plays in Glück's poetry. Together they interpret how Glück's voice modulates and the import of that modulation. Such change, moreover, must be based upon a sense of freedom, a belief in the possibility of approaching language and the world differently. One way for us to conceptualize this freedom is to envision Glück's poems as forming a kind of empathic witnessing, the testimony I allude to at the opening of this introduction. Such testimony evolves in Glück's work, I would suggest, from the early to the recent poems as Glück shifts the relation of speaker to subject, of text to reader. The capacity for change speaks to Glück's gifts, and the power of the witness increasingly gains nuance and flexibility. Glück's poems keep circling around the fundamental, existential issues that absorb each of us, but they do so in a way that transforms them into something other, into poetry that keeps remaking itself and therefore transcending the limitations of the real in order to create art.

NOTES

1. Shoshana Felman and Dori Laub, *Testimony: Crises of Witnessing in Literature, Psychoanalysis, and History* (New York: Routledge, 1992) 5.

2. *Proofs & Theories* (Hopewell, NJ: Ecco Press, 1994) 35. Subsequent references will appear in the text.

3. Helen Vendler, *Part of Nature, Part of Us: Modern American Poets* (Cambridge: Harvard University Press, 1980) 311.

4. *Descending Figure* is included in *The First Four Books of Poems* (Hopewell, NJ: Ecco Press, 1995).

Louise Glück

"I, with my inflexible Platonism, / my fierce seeing of only one thing at a time": a little collection could be made of the negative things that Glück has said about herself. This is not an attempt to charm; it is part of the poems' air of astringency, of applying the same disabused intelligence to the self that the self applies to the world.

An individual poem's decisive finality of structure, the *accent of fatality* characteristic of her lines, testifies to her seeing "one thing at a time" so profoundly that common seeing by comparison shrivels. On love:

> In his tent, Achilles
> grieved with his whole being
> and the gods saw
>
> he was a man already dead, a victim
> of the part that loved,
> the part that was mortal.
> —"The Triumph of Achilles"

Or:

> in childhood, I thought
> that pain meant
> I was not loved.
> It meant I loved.
>
> —"First Memory"

Or:

> We merely knew it wasn't human nature to love
> only what returns love.
>
> —"Matins"

Single poems, and finally whole volumes, invent brilliant, decisive structures to embody the decisive, singular things seen. Let the startling structure of the volume *The Wild Iris* stand for this: quickly the reader realizes that interspersed among other speakers flowers speak, telling their "being in the world" to their masters, human beings. Other poems are spoken by god, unheard by human beings who can apprehend him only through his creation, the natural world. Between the two are human speakers, who can clearly hear neither. The poet makes the reader privy to a vast hierarchic celestial conversation in which those who talk only dimly apprehend one other, a conversation which (fugue-like) intertwines identities that remain separate but whose coexistence sustains the grandeur and stability of the whole.

Balancing and fundamentally altering one's sense of this singularity of structure in individual poems and volumes is the protean, prodigal variety of Glück's "fierce seeing of only one thing at a time." The movement from poem to poem in *The Wild Iris* is nothing like that in the preceding volume, *Ararat*—and nothing like that in the volume that follows, *Meadowlands*. *Ararat* breathes the necessities, the bare-bones air of Greek tragedy; *Meadowlands* is modeled on "The Marriage of Figaro," with its human pathos, comedy, delight in invention of unexpected characters and contingent social texture. *Meadowlands* (1996) is part of the same enterprise as the next book, *Vita Nova* (1999). But because *Vita Nova* concentrates on the survival of the individual soul wounded by the events of *Meadowlands,* the social scene is gone: the book abjures the siren who began as a waitress as well as the shrewd ironies of Telemachus, substituting the severities of Dido and Eurydice. *Vita Nova*'s model is closer to the "Spiritual Exercises" of Loyola than to "Figaro." Then a gap: the latest volume, *The Seven Ages,* has leapt to a new, unexpected cave or eyrie on some cliff wall from which the poet can overlook the spectacle of human life. Three exhilarating books published from 1996 to 2001: five years of astonishing variety and invention.

No important word recurs more often in Glück's work than "form." She has a master's sense of form, and often meditates what necessities lie beneath shifts in form. She has a constantly fresh and unexpected way of *stationing* the self, the soul, vertically in relation to worlds above or below it, to its past or impending future. Let the ending of "Formaggio" stand for this recurrent gesture of *stationing* that frees the soul from the horizontal social world of observation and contingency, into a vertical world where the orders that define the soul's nature can shift throughout her work:

> I had lives before this, stems
> of a spray of flowers: they became
> one thing, held by a ribbon at the center, a ribbon
> visible under the hand. Above the hand,
> the branching future, stems
> ending in flowers. And the gripped fist—
> that would be the self in the present.

This *stationing* is not present in her first book, *Firstborn;* she began with the language and gestures contemporary poetry offered her (in this case, mostly the Lowell of *Lord Weary's Castle* and the first part of *Life Studies*). *Firstborn* is certainly talented, but in the five years before her next book, she remakes herself. She begins to discover a resonance unindebted to the dominant styles of the time, her characteristic accent of savage insight into fatality, though not yet purified of rhetoric: "This is the barrenness / of harvest or pestilence" ("All Hallows"). The discovery will be complete by the third book, *Descending Figure:* "I sleep so you will be alive, / it is that simple" ("The Dream of Mourning"). Reading through Glück's first books, you can watch her mastery grow in joining poem by poem; by *Ararat,* she has learned to make an entire book one sequence. Every subsequent book is a single emotional and intellectual arc—without the circumstantiality of the "confessional," they offer extraordinary candor about the poem's intimate life, the state of the soul.

I have just had one of the greatest experiences that contemporary writing can offer, which I recommend to you: over the course of two weeks read Louise Glück's nine books of poetry, in the order in which she published them.

WAYNE KOESTENBAUM

Introduction to a Reading

It is a deep honor to introduce Louise Glück, an indispensable poet in my reading and writing life, a poet I turn to for primary sustenance and inspiration. I cannot imagine the world of contemporary poetry without Glück's work, which is a way of saying that without her work I cannot imagine the world. For twenty years I have been listening to Louise Glück's poems for lessons in some of the cardinal literary virtues, which include, foremost, the shunning of virtuosity; her work is, in my estimation, not merely poetry, but pedagogy, creed, philosophy—a set of daunting, shining standards that we as readers should strive to live up to, however much we will fail. (Her poems never fail, but always concern failure, and forgive it.) Her poems are concise, precise, hard, reticent, unsentimental, spare. Their spareness does not preclude comedy; their reticence does not prohibit elevation. Their mode is declaration, not description. Their goal is the purveying of "high-quality information": as Glück says of Emily Dickinson, in an essay, "We trust the poem regardless, since we trust high-quality information."

What information do Glück's poems purvey? The news that human relations are fraught; that trauma is speech's backbone; that happiness depends on a deep apprenticeship in misery; that desires obey primal, unrevisable laws; that the heavenly powers are stingy; that most speech is a lie. The context of Glück's poems—the context they work *against,* as nervy antidote—is what Tennessee Williams called "mendacity"; Glück's poems assume a preemptive, hostile world in which everyone will interrupt her, strive to complete (and negate) her sentences, undercut her independence, cause her to cower. Against these workaday brutalities, she proposes, in her poems, a set of elementary theorems, passports to sanity: that speech is appetite; that appetites are cannibalistic (no sense denying it!); that words are actions; and that we have no time for décor.

Glück's poems are perfectly graceful exemplars of high artful-

From a reading at the 92nd Street Y, New York City, February 4, 2002.

ness, but that is not why I revere them; I revere them because they sting, and because, like those of her great predecessors in the pursuit of the minimalist ecstatic (Sappho, Dickinson, Cavafy, Oppen, Éluard, Ponge), Glück's poems are too busy relaxing after having just barely escaped annihilation to bother about being charming, chatty, or anecdotal. Their business—their *idée fixe*—is permanence, and they reach that state of no-bleed color-fast fixity by exercising a riveting stare. Her poems mimic the undead shield; they plan to stop time, even at the cost of iconoclasm. (And "poetry" is the first of the icons to be shattered.)

Many of us who write poems try to stuff them with "proof" that we are, indeed, poets, as if we didn't trust the vocation's self-evidence. Glück's poems, in contrast, bring no energy of special pleading or underconfident showmanship to the table; quietly Mallarmean, they are as purely "poem" as anything that has been written in the last half century. They are poems not because they are trying obsequiously or arrogantly to prove they are poems, but because they have no choice but to be poems. They choose "poem" not because it is a comfortable identity, but because it is the damaged identity, leaving no physical traces after the eviscerating, self-shattering act of articulation.

Her poems assert that to speak is to be horrified. Any serious contemporary thinking about discourse will need to listen closely to Glück's work, an important array of evidence that language, in our culture, has *not* been cheapened to the point of dirt, and that, indeed, silences in a conflicted utterance can still, amid postmodernity's roar, be heard.

LINDA GREGERSON

The Sower against Gardens

The gods, that mortal beauty chase,
Still in a tree did end their race.
—ANDREW MARVELL, "THE GARDEN"

Louise Glück is one of those enviable poets whose powers and distinction emerged early and were early recognized. Her work has
been justly admired and justly influential, as only work of the very
first order can be: work so impeccably itself that it alters the landscape in which others write while at the same time discouraging
(and dooming) the ordinary homage of direct imitation. In 1992
Glück published a sixth book and in 1996 a seventh which, in their
sustained engagement with inherited fable and inherited form, in
their simultaneously witty and deadly serious subversions, constitute a deepening so remarkable that it amounts to a new departure.
These books are unlike one another in any number of outward dis-
positions, but they share a common intellectual purchase; they are
two poles of a single project.

1. Like Me

The Wild Iris makes its entrance late in the life of a tradition and its
self-wrought woes: the moral and aesthetic dilemmas of sentimental projection, the metaphysical dilemma of solitude (if the others
with whom I am in dialogue are merely the projections of self, I am
alone in the world, and, worse, the world has been lost on me). The
poet plants herself in a garden and dares its other Creator to join
her. The poet construes her garden to be an anthropomorphic
thicket and a series of moral exempla. The poet ventriloquizes all the
voices—floral, human, transcendent—in a family quarrel about love
and sustenance. With equal portions of bravura and self-deprecation,

From the *Kenyon Review* 23 (winter 2001): 115–33.

wit and rue, *The Wild Iris* mindfully renders its dilemmas by means of an interwoven series of dramatic monologues. These have, some of them, been published separately (they are poems of great individual beauty), but they are not separable: the book is a single meditation that far exceeds its individual parts.

The monologues are of three sorts: (1) those spoken by a human persona to God, or to that which holds the place of God; (2) those spoken by the botanical inhabitants of the garden cultivated by the human persona; and (3) those spoken by divinity. The poems addressed to God take their titles and their rhetorical premise from the Christian canonical hours (here reduced from seven to two), which mark the daily cycles of prayer. The poems spoken by flowers, groundcover, and one flowering tree take their color and argument from the circumstances of individual species (annuals vs. perennials, shade plants vs. sun plants, single blossoms vs. multiple); excluded from voicing are only those vegetable denizens identified with human "use" or consumption. The God-voiced poems take their titles from the saturating conditions of nature: weather, season, the qualities of wind or light. The poet is clearly aware that her central device, the affective identification that characterizes so large a portion of nature poetry in English, has sometimes borne the stigma of "fallacy," so she incorporates a preemptive ironist:

> The sun shines; by the mailbox, leaves
> of the divided birch tree folded, pleated like fins.
> Underneath, hollow stems of the white daffodils,
>   Ice Wings, Cantatrice; dark
> leaves of the wild violet. Noah says
> depressives hate the spring, imbalance
> between the inner and the outer world. I make
> another case—being depressed, yes, but in a sense passionately
> attached to the living tree, my body
> actually curled in the split trunk, almost at peace,
>   in the evening rain
> almost able to feel
> sap frothing and rising: Noah says this is
> an error of depressives, identifying
> with a tree, whereas the happy heart
> wanders the garden like a falling leaf, a figure for
> the part, not the whole.

>   —"Matins"

If we are paying attention, we can discern the season before Noah names it: daffodils are a spring flower; the leaves of the birch tree are as yet unfolded. But the foreboding that attaches to the season is entirely inexplicit until Noah is made to comment upon it and, commenting, to deflate it. "Entirely" is perhaps misleading. In situ, in the full *Wild Iris,* some portion of foreboding inevitably infects this poem by way of the poem that immediately precedes it. In that previous poem, which is also the title poem, the awakening rendered in the voice of an iris is a transition of stirring beauty ("from the center of my life came / a great fountain, deep blue / shadows on azure seawater") and intractable pain ("It is terrible to survive / as consciousness / buried in the dark earth"). But that which is metaphysical in "The Wild Iris" and mythic in the mind of the "Matins" speaker (notice her partial invocation of Daphne) is in Noah's breezy analysis a thing considerably more banal. Instead of ontology, the garden's resident ironist discerns psychology; instead of tragic insight, the symptomatic "presentation" of temperament or disease. This witty, transient, pathologizing of point of view produces a marvelous mobility of tone, a mobility manifest in local instances of Glück's earlier work but never so richly developed as in the present volume. And never so strategically important. By anticipating and incorporating the skeptical reader, by fashioning the poetic sequence as a dialogue with disbelief, the speaker procures considerable license for her extravagant impersonations: of violets; of witchgrass; of Eve in the Garden; nay, of God. We find early on that we will grant this speaker any number of investigations-by-means-of-likeness. And why? Because we like her.

God and the flowers speak with the voice of the human; the human writer has no other voice to give them. The flowers sense, or describe sensation, in unabashedly human terms: "I feel it / glinting through the leaves," says the shaded vine, "like someone hitting the side of a glass with a metal spoon" ("Lamium"). They measure aptitude by contrast or analogy with human aptitude: "things / that can't move," says the rooted tree, "learn to see; I do not need / to chase you through / the garden" ("The Hawthorne Tree"); "I am not like you," says the rose, "I have only / my body for a voice" ("The White Rose"). God speaks in the voice of an earthly parent who has reached the end of his tether: "How can I help you when you all want / different things" ("Midsummer"); "Do you suppose I care / if you speak to one another?" ("April").

God explains himself by analogy and contradistinction to the human: "I am not like you in this, / I have no release in another body" ("End of Summer"). God, like his creatures, assumes the simplifying contours of the familial: "You were like very young children, / always waiting for a story. . . . / I was tired of telling stories" ("Retreating Light").

But likeness marks an irreparable chasm as well:

> So I gave you the pencil and paper.
> I gave you pens made of reeds
> I had gathered myself, afternoons in the dense meadows.
> I told you, write your own story.
> . . . .
> Then I realized you couldn't think
> with any real boldness or passion;
> you hadn't had your own lives yet,
> your own tragedies.
> So I gave you lives, I gave you tragedies,
> because apparently tools alone weren't enough.
>
> You will never know how deeply
> it pleases me to see you sitting there
> like independent beings . . .
>
> —"Retreating Light"

That "like" is ice to the heart. Those who achieve authentic independence require no "like."

Shadowing this book is the troubling possibility, indeed, the certain knowledge, that its analogies are false or partial. "Whatever you hoped," says God in the voice of the wind, "you will not find yourselves in the garden, / among the growing plants. / Your lives are not circular like theirs" ("Retreating Wind"). Worse yet from the poet's perspective, her analogies may be forced: "if this were not a poem but / an actual garden," one skeptical interlocutor opines, "then / the red rose would be / required to resemble / nothing else, neither / another flower nor / the shadowy heart" ("Song"). Our Renaissance forebears had a term for the clothing of divinity in earthly garments: they called this process "accommodation." Because we are weak, because we cannot behold divinity face to face, God "accommodates" himself to our limits, agreeing to be known by elements available to human sense. These measures, however, are imperfect and interim:

> I've submitted to your preferences, observing patiently
> the things you love, speaking
>
> through vehicles only, in
> details of earth, as you prefer,
>
> tendrils
> of blue clematis, light
>
> of early evening—
> you would never accept
>
> a voice like mine, indifferent
> to the objects you busily name,
>
> your mouths
> small circles of awe—
>
> And all this time
> I indulged your limitation. . . .
>
> —"Clear Morning"

Glück's couplets do not in any straightforward sense coincide with the divisions of dialogue, but they do, subtly, remind us that accommodation is a two-part contract. God's patience is not infinite: "I cannot go on / restricting myself to images // because you think it is your right / to dispute my meaning" ("Clear Morning"). In order to grant his creatures an interim meeting place, the Creator agrees to interim diminishment. But this delicate contract breaks down the minute it is presumed upon:

> You were not intended
> to be unique. You were
> my embodiment, all diversity
>
> not what you think you see
> searching the bright sky over the field,
> your incidental souls
> fixed like telescopes on some
> enlargement of yourselves—
>
> —"Midsummer"

Do not flatter yourselves, the Creator warns. Despite what you imagine, what I allow you for a time to imagine, I am not like you.

2. We

And you are plural. You are mere repetitive examples, as the crowd beneath your feet can witness:

> Not I, you idiot, not self, but we, we—waves
> of sky blue like
> a critique of heaven: why
> do you treasure your voice
> when to be one thing
> is to be next to nothing?
> Why do you look up? To hear
> an echo like the voice
> of god?
>
> —"Scilla"

The plural pronoun is a reproach to vanity, and in *The Wild Iris* it issues not only from below but from above as well, and in the harsher second person:

> You wanted to be born; I let you be born.
> When has my grief ever gotten
> in the way of your pleasure?
>
> Plunging ahead
> . . . .
> as though you were some new thing, wanting
> to express yourselves
> . . . .
>
> never thinking
> this would cost you anything,
> never imagining the sound of my voice
> as anything but part of you—
>
> —"End of Winter"

The accusatory mode is one the human persona can adopt as well. "[H]ow can I live / in colonies, as you prefer," she asks, "if you impose / a quarantine of affliction, dividing me / from healthy members of / my own tribe" ("Matins"). This counter-complaint, with its foundational recourse to a singular self, is all the more credible for missing the point. But the leverage inherent in the first-person plural has not been entirely lost on the human speaker; she too can manipulate the moral advantage in numbers when she will: "Unreachable father, when we were first / exiled from heaven, you made / a replica, a place in one sense / different from heaven, being / designed to teach a lesson" ("Matins"). In one sense, the speaker's imperturbable assumptions about didactic function are simply another manifestation of self-regard: the garden cannot simply be; the garden must mean; it was made *for me*. And though the speaker describes an affliction shared with others, or one particular other, of her kind, the shared aptitude appears to be for solitude: "Left alone, / we exhausted each other" ("Matins"). What lifts these passages above the common run of vanity is the ground of knowing they describe: "We never thought of you / whom we were learning to worship. / We merely knew it wasn't human nature to love / only what returns love" ("Matins"). In *The Wild Iris* as in its dominant line of lyric forebears, unrequited longing is the constitutive feature of consciousness. The garden is a sign because it is redolent with absence. The sharers in the garden come to know themselves by knowing that something is missing; their very failure to sustain one another is part of the message.

Given all this absence, what may we infer about the Maker? He has absconded. His voice is the "persistent echoing / in all sound that means good-bye, good-bye— / the one continuous line / that binds us to each other" ("End of Winter"). The "we" that includes deity is a "we" shot through with departure, so in his leaving, the deity has left us one another, another "we." And how have we made use of this solace?

> No one's despair is like my despair—
>
> You have no place in this garden
> thinking such things, producing
> the tiresome outward signs; the man
> pointedly weeding an entire forest,
> the woman limping, refusing to change clothes
> or wash her hair.

Do you suppose I care
if you speak to one another?
But I mean you to know
I expected better of two creatures
who were given minds: if not
that you would actually care for each other
at least that you would understand
grief is distributed
between you, among all your kind, for me
to know you, as deep blue
marks the wild scilla, white
the wood violet.

—"April"

The irritable reaching after uniqueness ("No one's despair is like my despair") has taken its toll on human community. Despair has become for the couple in the garden a competitive pastime. But behind the orthodox proposition that despair is a species of pride, self-made and self-sustained, lies a yet more chilling possibility: what if we are on to the truth in spite of ourselves? What if grief is indeed our only claim to distinction? When the biblical faithful are forced to consider that their ends may not be coincident with the ends of the Creator, they have generally contrived to find this difference reassuring: God knows better; God makes us suffer for our own good. But what if God doesn't know better at all? Or what if his knowing doesn't have much to do with us? What if, except for our suffering, God could not tell us apart?

The distributed personae of *The Wild Iris* think through to the other side of this all-but-unthinkable proposition from time to time, think beyond the obvious panic such a proposition induces, and address deity as another of the vulnerable species of creation:

        —I am ashamed
at what I thought you were,
distant from us, regarding us
as an experiment
. . . .
            . . . Dear friend,
dear trembling partner, what
surprises you most in what you feel,
earth's radiance or your own delight?

—"Matins"

This is not the voice of first, or naive, intimacy, not the voice of the child who takes for granted that the parent is near, but the voice of willed, or revisionist, intimacy, the voice of the adult who has wearied of blame. It is a voice that may be adopted not only by the privileged species for whom the garden was created but also, and with equal eloquence, by the garden's humblest residents:

> Because in our world
> something is always hidden,
> small and white,
> small and what you call
> pure, we do not grieve
> as you grieve, dear
> suffering master; you
> are no more lost
> than we are, under
> the hawthorn tree, the hawthorn holding
> balanced trays of pearls: what
> has brought you among us
> who would teach you, though
> you kneel and weep,
> clasping your great hands,
> in all your greatness knowing
> nothing of the soul's nature,
> which is never to die: poor sad god,
> either you never have one
> or you never lose one.
>
> —"Violets"

Nowhere in this limpid book does its triangular logic emerge with greater resonance. The human addresses God for the most part; the flowers and God address the human. And sometimes, to the flowers, the human appears in the guise of God, as flawed as the God to whom humans turn. But where is the human in "Violets"? Between "our world" and "your great hands," the human may be present, for once, chiefly by omission. And the posited soul: how is it that the violets know it? Do they have a soul? Does God? Does one have to have a soul in order to know the nature of the soul? Or does one know the nature of the soul only from the outside, only by being without one? Are we to imagine that the poor sad god in the garden grieves at being without a soul? Or does he grieve because he is unable to be rid of the soul? The only point on which the violets appear to speak unambiguously, a point quite devastating enough, is that grieving will not *make* a soul.

We three then: the two in dialogue and the one just beyond the bounds of dialogue, in whom the dialogue is grounded. The triangular manipulation of presence is as old as the lyric itself. He who sits beside you, writes Sappho. She that hath you, Shakespeare writes. Jealousy stands for but also masks a more frightening possibility. "Much / has passed between us," writes Glück; "Or / was it always only / on the one side?" ("Matins").

3. Reciprocal

The spectral possibility that gives lyric its urgency is not that the beloved isn't listening, but that the beloved doesn't exist. Prayer takes place at the edge of a similar abyss:

> Once I believed in you; I planted a fig tree.
> Here, in Vermont, country
> of no summer. It was a test: if the tree lived,
> it would mean you existed.
>
> By this logic, you do not exist. Or you exist
> exclusively in warmer climates,
> in fervent Sicily and Mexico and California,
> where are grown the unimaginable
> apricot and fragile peach. Perhaps
> they see your face in Sicily; here, we barely see
> the hem of your garment. I have to discipline myself
> to share with John and Noah the tomato crop.
>
> —"Vespers"

The poet's logic here is that of clever blackmail. God won't show? Perhaps he can be taunted into breaking cover. The speaker plants a fig tree, or the story of a fig tree, as a dare. When the fig tree predictably dies, the dare modulates to witty demotion. Are you not here, father? Perhaps you are somewhere else? Or perhaps you are littler than we thought. To propose that God might "exist exclusively in warmer climates" is to bait a withholding deity: it goes without saying that God can be no God unless he is everywhere at once. Or does it? Perhaps the absurdity cuts both ways. Perhaps comedic gesture throws into relief the deep peculiarity of an all-or-nothing system that is premised on "jealousy." A jealous God gets the jealous children ("I have to discipline myself," etc.) he deserves:

> If there is justice in some other world, those
> like myself, whom nature forces
> into lives of abstinence, should get
> the lion's share of all things, all
> objects of hunger, greed being
> praise of you. And no one praises
> more intensely than I, with more
> painfully checked desire, or more deserves
> to sit at your right hand, if it exists, partaking
> of the perishable, the immortal fig,
> which does not travel.
>
> —"Vespers"

Gospel has promised that the poor shall possess the kingdom of heaven, and the poet wants her share, "the lion's share," of this compensatory promotion. Far from admitting greed as grounds for penance, she brazenly advances greed as the badge of special comprehension and thus of special dessert. If God has bounty to dispense, then perhaps, like other patrons, he may be bribed. Praise is the coinage of patronage, whose darker side is "if." "If there is justice in some other world": the conditional clause says justice in the present world has fallen short. "[I]f it exists": the conditional clause insinuates that part of the power, and part of the power to judge, resides with the believer. If the Father, in order to exist, requires our faith as we require his bounty, we may have found the key to reciprocal consent. But lest the contract prove too dry, the poet does not stop here, does not pause too long to congratulate herself for unmasking the circular structure of vested interest. She returns instead to the object that passes between the master and the lovers in the garden, that makes the longing palpable, or nearly so: the promised, the withheld, the here-and-absent fig.

For the lover is a gardener too:

> In your extended absence, you permit me
> use of earth, anticipating
> some return on investment.
>
> —"Vespers"

This gardener glances obliquely at the parable of the talents (see Matthew 25; see Milton's nineteenth sonnet). It is a useful parable, invoking spiritual and mercenary economies in unseemly proximity. Unseemliness prompts resistance, a common heuristic device. It also prompts reproach:

> I must report
> failure in my assignment, principally
> regarding the tomato plants.
>
> —"Vespers"

Adopting the disconsonant diction of spreadsheet and quarterly report, the gardener achieves a wicked deadpan, fair warning that she does not intend to shoulder the failure alone:

> I think I should not be encouraged to grow
> tomatoes. Or, if I am, you should withhold
> the heavy rains, the cold nights that come
> so often here, while other regions get
> twelve weeks of summer.
>
> —"Vespers"

The multiplying indecorums now include domestic comedy. The disgruntled dependent resourcefully finds that she is not to blame after all, that someone else has caused her fault, someone whose crime is the misapportionment of original love. And then, apparent concession: "All this / belongs to you." But the concession is quickly withdrawn:

> All this
> belongs to you: on the other hand,
> I planted the seeds, I watched the first shoots
> like wings tearing the soil, and it was my heart
> broken by the blight, the black spot so quickly
> multiplying in the rows. I doubt
> you have a heart, in our understanding of
> that term. You who do not discriminate
> between the dead and the living, who are, in consequence,
> immune to foreshadowing, you may not know
> how much terror we bear, the spotted leaf,
> the red leaves of the maple falling

even in August, in early darkness: I am responsible
for these vines.

—"Vespers"

The hilarious, instantaneous taking back of that which was fleetingly granted—God's proprietary interest in creation—begins in
petulance: mine, says the poet; the suffering is mine. But petulance
expands to a countercharge—you have no heart—that bit by bit
accumulates plausibility. God's loftier perspective, his comprehensive vision, begins to look like insufficiency. For comprehensiveness
is by its very nature incapable of something too, incapable of "fore-
shadowing," of temporal habitation, of partialness and partiality, the
realms of feeling possessed by those who are subject to time. Unfolding these realms, the human voice becomes tutelary, makes
concession to the newly contemplated incapacities of deity: "you
may not know."

And then the inventory of terror: the spotted leaf, the falling
leaf, the early darkness. And, signaled by the colon, the syllogistic
revelation: I am the only one left to be responsible. The line is not
merely syllogistic, of course. Spoken within the parameters of apos-
trophic address, and spoken to one who might have been assumed
to be responsible himself, it is a reprimand: unlike you, I take my
responsibilities to heart. The reprimand is also a piece of games-
manship, another in the series of rhetorical moves designed to flush
God out. By what standard may we judge its success? God has not,
we must confess, been coerced into unambiguous manifestation.
On the other hand, the game has not quite stalled. For even as the
speaker makes her sinuous case for self, something beyond the
self—a "we" who bear the terror, the vines—has claimed the self's
attention. This may be small. It is certainly strategic. But even in the
momentary, the strategic assumption of responsibility, the self ac-
crues a new degree of moral dignity. This moment may be as close
as God will come.

In poem after poem, *The Wild Iris* delineates a reciprocal drawing out of spirit. This is not to say it is a sanguine book:

> Sometimes a man or woman forces his despair
> on another person, which is called
> baring the heart, alternatively, baring the soul—
> meaning for this moment they acquired souls—
>
> —"Love in Moonlight"

Moonlight is reflected light, light "taken from another source," and love in this light a kind of violent seizing, or theft. The God who may or may not exist may take his logic from moonlight or love or, failing that, from parables. "You are perhaps training me to be / responsive to the slightest brightening," the poet ventures. "Or, like the poets, / are you stimulated by despair?" ("Vespers"). The poet takes a walk at sunset in the company of her despair. And in helpless arousal or deliberate grace, in one of two contrary modes, the God she refuses to look for appears:

> As you anticipated,
> I did not look up. So you came down to me:
> at my feet, not the wax
> leaves of the wild blueberry but your fiery self, a whole
> pasture of fire, and beyond, the red sun neither falling
> nor rising—
> I was not a child; I could take advantage of illusions.
>
> —"Vespers"

This final resolution might be epigraph to the entire book of the garden.

4. Domestic

The domestic comedy that offers counterpoint to metaphysical debate in *The Wild Iris* assumes center stage in *Meadowlands,* the book of poems Glück published four years later. In this new book, the garden has given way to landscape of a different sort: the grasslands behind a childhood home on Long Island or surrounding the home of a twenty-year marriage in Vermont, the grasslands long buried beneath a football stadium in industrial New Jersey. Glück's subject has long been the zero-sum game of the nuclear family (even when she grants a place to grandparents, aunts, and a sister's children, they are merely the reiterative instances of nuclear entrapment). The wit and the paradox, the razor-edge renderings of human motivation and human stalemate, have been in place for decades. But now they are fresher, deeper than ever before. What has moved the project forward so dramatically is a structural insight: the deployment of inherited patterns (devotional hours, growing season, garden epic, voyage epic, scripts for different voices) on a book-length scale. Like

The Wild Iris, Meadowlands has been constructed as a single argument, internally cross-referenced, dramatically unified. Its story is the breakdown of a marriage, and its template is Homeric.

What has the marriage in *Meadowlands* to do with the story of Odysseus and Penelope? Its time span is roughly twenty years, divided into two decade-long segments, one of them "happy." Its measure is roughly the span of a young son's growing into manhood, and judgment, and ironic commentary. Its outward incidents are driven by a husband's appetite for adventure. Its deeper momentum derives from the tension between excursus and domesticity. But the template yields rich results precisely because its fit is only approximate:

> Little soul
>   . . . He will be home soon;
> it behooves you to be
> generous. You have not been completely
> perfect either; with your troublesome body
> you have done things you shouldn't
> discuss in poems. Therefore
> call out to him over the open water, over the bright water
> with your dark song, with your grasping,
> unnatural song—passionate,
> like Maria Callas. Who
> wouldn't want you? Whose most demonic appetite
> could you possibly fail to answer? Soon
> he will return from wherever he goes in the meantime,
> suntanned from his time away, wanting
> his grilled chicken. Ah, you must greet him,
> you must shake the boughs of the tree
> to get his attention,
> but carefully, carefully, lest
> his beautiful face be marred
> by too many falling needles.
>   —"Penelope's Song"

If the second Homeric epic has held enduring appeal for female narrators, this surely has something to do with Penelope's leveraged position in a complex economy of desire. The human heroines of the *Iliad* are essentially single-function figures, the bearers of prophecy, grief, beauty, and fidelity in a world whose primary contests—erotic, political, martial—are waged by men. But Penelope's position is sustained by ambiguities as rich as those that sustain Achilles. She weaves a shroud for a patriarch who is not yet dead; she rules a royal household, albeit in a compromised and declining state, during the prolonged absence of her husband and the minority of her son; she entertains a populous band of suitors whose extended address makes her uniquely immune to the erosions of age. Penelope has every reason to delay, and the reader has every reason to lodge in her vicinity. Her cup is never empty, her position ever summary: wife, mother, queen, perpetual subject of desire. If the quality of that desire is somewhat clouded by a husband's waywardness and the suitors' greed and boorishness, its breadth and duration are nevertheless the stuff of fantasy. Finally, crucially, Penelope's composite position makes her a center of consciousness, something to which not even the paragon Helen may aspire.

"[B]ut carefully, carefully, lest / his beautiful face be marred / by too many falling needles." The poet wears her mythic trappings lightly when it suits her: the frank anachronisms of Maria Callas and grilled chicken are fair indicators. The falling needles of a pine tree may be the poem's only, oblique allusion to the heroine's cloth-working artistry, which signifies retirement (the upstairs loom) and an aptitude for aggression (some damage to the hero's face). The framework of *Meadowlands* will open to admit any number of irreverent intrusions from late in the second millennium: a dishwasher, a purple bathing suit, the neighbors' klezmer band, a resolute vernacular. Nor are the book's mythic templates exclusively Homeric: one poem draws its title and its premise (the ordinary miracle of marriage) from the wedding at Cana; one is addressed to the serpent of Genesis; several make of birds and beasts and flowering plants a built-to-purpose parable. Narrative foundations are overlapping and distillate: the wife divides her perspective among several alter egos, several island wives, including her chief rival, Circe. The husband's reiterated departure seems sometimes to be his departure from the modern marriage, sometimes the infidelities that prepare for that departure, sometimes Odysseus's departure for Troy, sometimes his serial departures on the homeward trip to Ithaca, sometimes the shadowy final departure rehearsed in epic continuations like the *Inferno* or the lost *Telegonia*.[1]

The great advantage of broad outline is its suppleness, its freedom from clutter:

The Greeks are siting on the beach
wondering what to do when the war ends. No one
wants to go home, back
to that bony island; everyone wants a little more
of what there is in Troy, more
life on the edge, that sense of every day as being
packed with surprises. But how to explain this
to the ones at home to whom
fighting a war is a plausible
excuse for absence, whereas
exploring one's capacity for diversion
is not.

—"Parable of the Hostages"

This freedom from clutter is a rhetorical talent shared by Telemachus, whose earlier incarnation was as Noah in *The Wild Iris*.
Telemachus has learned that ironists need never be out of work:

When I was a child looking
at my parents' lives, you know
what I thought? I thought
heartbreaking. Now I think
heartbreaking, but also
insane. Also
very funny.

—"Telemachus' Detachment"

The domestic quarrel, with its soul-destroying pettiness and con-
volution, would seem to be inimical to lyric poetry. One of the
great technical triumphs of *Meadowlands* is to have found a form in
which the soul-destroying can be transmuted to the spirit-reviving.
The genius is not just in the leaving out, though elision is its indispensable method, but also in the undressed, unwashed leaving in:

Speak to me, aching heart: what
ridiculous errand are you inventing for yourself
weeping in the dark garage
with your sack of garbage: it is not your job
to take out the garbage, it is your job
to empty the dishwasher. You are showing off again, . . .

—"Midnight"

But Glück's finest formal innovation in this volume is reserved for the structure of domestic dialogue. She tracks the wild non sequitur, the sidestep and the feint, the ambush, the afterthought, the timed delay. As in Penelope's weaving, the thread that seemed to have been dropped resurfaces, having meanwhile lent its tensile continuity to the underside of the narrative:

> How could the Giants name
> that place the Meadowlands? It has
> about as much in common with a pasture
> as would the inside of an oven.

New Jersey
was rural. They want you
to remember that.

Simms
was not a thug. LT
was not a thug.

> What I think is we should
> look at our surroundings
> realistically, for what they are
> in the present.

That's what
I tell you about the house.

No giant
would talk the way you talk.
You'd be a nicer person
if you were a fan of something.
When you do that with your mouth
you look like your mother.

You know what they are?
Kings among men.

> So what king
> fired Simms?

—"Meadowlands 3"

Ten such dialogue poems appear in the course of *Meadowlands,* eleven if one counts, and one should, the epigraph. All are distinguished by the same minimalist annotation—the woman speaking in indented stanzas, the man flush left—and by a handful of recurrent themes. Once the convention and the leitmotifs have established themselves, the poet is free to begin and end in heady, hilarious medias res: three bare lines and a single speaker in "Meadowlands 2," another single speaker in "Void." No matter that the partner in speech is silent for the moment: these poems are cast as rejoinders and thus take part in a two-part song. Their workings are in situ, inseparable from the tonal and semantic resource of the book. Given the theme of the book, of course, this indissolubility of the whole achieves no little poignance. And greatly to its credit, it achieves delight. The reader is granted the pleasures of an initiate, one who knows the players without a scorecard, and the pleasures of an exuberant pace. No small prize to rescue from the ashes.

5. One

> *Let's play choosing music. Favorite form.*
> Opera.
> *Favorite work.*
>
> *Figaro. No. Figaro and Tannhauser. Now*
> *it's your turn: sing one for me.*
> —LOUISE GLÜCK,
> EPIGRAPH TO *MEADOWLANDS*

Mozart's is a comic opera of marriage. Wagner's is a tragic romance, in which the hero philanders and the heroine dies of a broken heart. Sing one, says the hero: make the one tradition comprehensive. Do the different voices, and make them add up to a whole. Sing for me: make me miss you when I am gone.

"[A] figure for / the part," said Noah in an earlier book. "[N]ot," he said, "the whole" ("Matins"). But his subject was the happy heart. Part of the wit that unites these books is their tracing of great epic themes—Milton's in the first instance, Homer's in the second—to their origins in the domestic. By means of this tracing they continue the logic already inherent in their lofty predecessors. But the latter-day garden and the meadowlands share another logic too, a logic more specific to the lyric. They posit conversation in a fertile world: my part, yours, the whole making more than the sum of its parts. And always they hear the conversation breaking down, the answer reduced to echo, the several voices to one. "The beloved doesn't / need to live," says the weaver in equal parts grimness and joy. "The beloved / lives in the head" ("Ithaca").

NOTE

1. The *Telegonia* (sixth century B.C.E.) takes its name from Telegonus, son of Odysseus and Circe. On the structural kinship and durable erotic powers of rival women, this lost epic was apparently superb: its plot is said to have included the ultimate marriage of Circe to Telemachus and of Penelope to Telegonus, two mothers to two sons. Odysseus had by this time succumbed.

Meadowlands
Trustworthy Speakers

In *Ararat* Louise Glück gives us a version of the Cretan Liar Paradox: "Don't listen to me; my heart's been broken. / I don't see anything objectively." The poem is called "The Untrustworthy Speaker," but of course we do listen and we do trust, because the poet knows her own distortions and because distortions, ordered by art, reveal what is hidden by the normative. Glück is enough of a modernist to believe in a separation of personality and artistic genius. The artist uses the self as a "lightning rod" of experience (*Proofs & Theories,* 45), but then gathers that energy into the production of a truth which is not exclusively of experience or of the self. That untrustworthy speaker can be traced to Glück's earliest volume, though she has only gradually been mastered by the trustworthy poet. Much of the energy of Glück's early work comes from its way of understanding everything in terms of the self, and therefore identifying poetic truth with self-absorption. And what else should we expect from a firstborn? But early on, too, Glück labored toward another kind of truth, introducing alternative standards of measurement, and artistic methods—description, myth, persona—that involved detours from the circle of self-regard. In *Meadowlands* that detour has turned onto a whole new landscape, where narrative and dialogue expand the vista of the lyric. The speakers of *Meadowlands* are not objective—they grieve, rage, seduce, betray—but in the disciplined world of the poems they are trustworthy.

Broken hearts and broken minds speak to us throughout *Firstborn.*[1] The title poem compels us to its vision, not through fairness but through hyperbole. It is the mid-1960s, and Plath's powerful overstatement is the dominant aesthetic, exposing the grotesque underside of domestic routine. Glück's speaker, indistinguishable from the poet, portrays herself as victim, others as unconscious betrayers:

The weeks go by. I shelve them,
They are all the same, like peeled soup cans . . .
Beans sour in their pot. I watch the lone onion
Floating like Ophelia, caked with grease:
You listless, fidget with the spoon.
What now? You miss my care? Your yard ripens
To a ward of roses, like a year ago when staff nuns
Wheeled me down the aisle . . .
You couldn't look. I saw
Converted love, your son,
Drooling under glass, starving . . .

We are eating well.
Today my meatman turns his trained knife
On veal, your favorite. I pay with my life.

While there is much to admire in the eruption of metaphor
here, the mature poet of *Meadowlands* (or any of the subsequent
volumes) has rejected this stance, in which others are mere sound-
ings of the self's dissatisfaction. The poem attempts to preserve an
innocent, sensitive self, one that bears witness to and suffers from
the ostensibly tragic and violent events that disguise themselves in
the ordinary. The interior life of the speaker is invested in the sim-
iles and expanded by the ellipses, where it has no limits. In Plath
we often feel that the speaker gains some power through hyperbole, hurling it back at the world as a kind of victory of the imagination. Glück's speaker is not aggressive in this way, only passive-
aggressive. She suffers and pays; she does not create these images.
And it isn't clear to whom she is bearing witness. The you might
be the husband (there is plenty of anger at men in this book), or
a part of the self that has yielded to the demands of the physical
and social world, the well-fed housewife who pays with her starving soul. Both partner and experiential self are split from a private
self that suffers from corrupted or neglected affection, turning up
in objective correlatives like "the lone onion / Floating like
Ophelia" and the starving baby, commodified and untouchable
"under glass." Yet the author seems wholly identified with the pro-
jector of these nerves upon a screen. One hears James Wright's
style of sincerity (that is, a style borrowed from Rilke) in "I pay
with my life." Untrustworthy speakers, modernism has shown, can
be the most interesting, but only (as in Prufrock) when their part

in the formation of their responses is revealed. Here that part remains unacknowledged, unexamined.

By contrast, "Penelope's Song," from *Meadowlands,* is alert to motive and wary of histrionics, without retreating into a bland objectivity. On the contrary, Penelope's subjectivity is the focus of the poem, which is addressed to the soul, now exposed to scrutiny:

> Little soul, little perpetually undressed one,
> do now as I bid you, climb
> the shelf-like branches of the spruce tree;
> wait at the top, attentive, like
> a sentry or look-out. He will be home soon;
> it behooves you to be
> generous. You have not been completely
> perfect either; with your troublesome body
> you have done things you shouldn't
> discuss in poems. Therefore
> call out to him over the open water, over the bright water
> with your dark song, with your grasping,
> unnatural song—passionate,
> like Maria Callas. Who
> wouldn't want you? Whose most demonic appetite
> could you possibly fail to answer? Soon
> he will return from wherever he goes in the meantime,
> suntanned from his time away, wanting
> his grilled chicken. Ah, you must greet him,
> you must shake the boughs of the tree
> to get his attention,
> but carefully, carefully, lest
> his beautiful face be marred
> by too many falling needles.

Penelope is recognizable as a middle-aged version of the speaker in "Firstborn." But the voice is modulated and the I/you split less absolute, thus less protective of private innocence. Penelope is also waiting, is also shelving her soul, not by peeling soup cans but, through allusion, by weaving and unweaving to bide her time. The speaker is not the soul, but one who must accommodate the claims of the soul to those of actuality. If the soul is the "little perpetually undressed one," its sincerity is displaced by a speaker who must master the will and control desire, in life and in art. For the minute the soul enters language, we know, it dresses itself up. It is indeed theatrical and would array itself as Maria Callas might for *Norma,* enraptured by the sound of its own dark song and presuming the power of that song over others. But the larger-than-life passions of the soul must meet the shrunken circumstances of the actual world in which the speaker lives. If one anticipates the meatman's "trained knife" of "Firstborn" in Penelope's projection of a lover with a "demonic appetite," one recognizes, on approach, that all he really wants is his "grilled chicken," undressed by metaphor, not the young flesh of veal. The speaker checks the soul's overstatement even as she respects its emotional extremes. What can it mean to be abject over so diminished a presence, "suntanned from his time away," his wickedness simply a boyish sense of adventure? It is not that the complaints of the soul are invalidated. Its grasping song still has the power to bring down the house, but life is not theater, at least not entirely. The grand gestures are absorbed into a compound syntax that reflects a complex motive. In contrast to "Firstborn," the violence that closes this poem is recognized as metaphor, indeed as pun, metaphor of the weakest kind. At the same time, it exposes, through understatement, a dark side to the speaker's control, the rage that lurks in the soul of the too generous, too faithful Penelope. This complexity has the further advantage of movement. The simple closing sentence in "Firstborn" produces a continuous, static present that can only repeat itself. "Penelope's Song" is full of the kind of conflict that produces rising action. A story is about to begin; our interest is therefore engaged, not only in the speaker's self but in the world and its changes.

Louise Glück has been reflecting, in her prose as well as in her verse, on this matter of trustworthy speakers. In "Against Sincerity" (*Proofs & Theories,* 33–45) she attempts to define, as exemplified in Berryman, an art involving the self and yet impersonal, negatively capable, or at least able to inhabit more than one perspective, to dramatize questions rather than project views. Shortly after the publication of *Meadowlands,* Glück wrote "American Narcissism,"[2] a kind of sequel to the earlier essay, and a study, in particular, of the literary effects and entrapments of self-regard. Only Rilke is explicitly condemned; one feels in the absence of specific targets not only tact but implicit self-criticism. As with most great poets, the sins she rails against are those of her youth: "In place of the will or appetite imposing itself on the world, or (as in Keats) the soul seeking, Rilke postulated a void, an absence into which the world flooded. The self was entirely reactive, so intensely so as to be exhausted by what, to a less scrupulous sensibility, would hardly be noticed." Glück's poetry understood this weakness and combated it long before her prose articulated it; her volumes can be read as a long labor to resist such hollowness. Glück's magnificent volume *The Wild Iris* represents her adventure in soul-seeking. In *Meadowlands* she examines the will and desire in the soul's encounters with other people. In both cases she recognizes the exploration of the self as lyric's great task, yet distinguishes it from a narcissism that refuses to delimit the self.

"American Narcissism" offers three strategies—actually effects managed through a variety of imaginative maneuvers—that discourage narcissistic entrapment: modesty, humor, and detachment. *Meadowlands* is a study of these, and all are present in "Penelope's Song." A modesty acknowledges: "You have not been completely / perfect either." Humor, operating often through shifts of discourse, reduces the "demonic appetite" to a craving for "grilled chicken." Detachment recognizes in the end that patience is a mask for rage, that the desire to attract (shaking the boughs) also involves the desire to wound (with the falling needles). These distancing devices do not erase the self; they create perspective that clarifies sight, as when we step back to see a detail of a painting in terms of the whole.

That whole is given in *Meadowlands* through the major *dramatis personae* of Homer's *Odyssey,* the ten years of Odysseus's journey conforming to a decade of modern marriage. We have not only the view of the abandoned wife, but also those of the male adventurer, the temptress, the son. This poet of lyric isolation has shown her chameleon colors. Glück's interest in retelling archetypal stories began long ago, but until now she has emphasized psychological depth or metaphysical reflection rather than dramatic possibility. Hence we have inconsolable anxiety in "Gretel in Darkness," the tragic convergence of beauty and violence in "Hyacinth." *Archaic Figure* emphasizes the iconic over the transformative. Here, by contrast, the individual voices become part of a larger story, a narrative, not just a psychomachia. There is something Greek, and fatalistic, in the encounters between the figures in this story. Each figure is rooted in an immovable passion, but the collision of these passions creates drama. If Penelope is the figure of devotion, domestic tranquility, and emotional generosity, Circe is not so much her rival as her other side: possessive will, bodily passion, jealousy that would "refuse you / sleep again / if I cannot have you" ("Circe's Torment"). It is a sign of Glück's modesty or at least her judiciousness that she does not give Odysseus a "song." He is a man of action and cunning, not of song, but besides this, he is the other, known only in a shadowy way. We get Odysseus's story impersonally, or in his interactions with Penelope, who replays his words. The most generous accounts of male motive come from Telemachus, whose distance is not a pale neutrality but a youthful investigation of adult possibilities and failures. He understands his father's "suffering, . . . a soul ardent by nature, thus ravaged by choice." Yet he recognizes in his mother "courage, subtly / expressed in inaction" ("Telemachus' Kindness"). At the same time, he sees their vanities. He is compassionate (the marriage is "heartbreaking"), analytical (the marriage is "insane"), and amused (the marriage is "very funny") ("Telemachus' Detachment"). He moves through kindness, guilt, dilemma, but ultimately detachment, the necessary transition of youth from its origins, those "opposing forces" of conjugal union. Telemachus adds an important possibility of movement within the depiction of immovable characters, for he at least has a future and can escape domestic gridlock.

This dramatic patterning of subjectivities is just one of the ways in which *Meadowlands* is Glück's most mimetic, and least Romantic, book. This mirror of life involves sacrifice that will disappoint some readers, attached to the stirring meditations of *The Triumph of Achilles* and *The Wild Iris,* with their figurative power and their sense of mystery. In the latter Glück offers a moving array of subjectivities, mostly nonhuman, that add not only perspective but height and depth to human life in its struggle with metaphysical questions. But that volume concerns the solitary life, in reflection and supplication, testing its defiance and submission. The self of *The Wild Iris* is contemplative, evoking and in turn refusing the divine within the cloistered world of the garden. The world Glück evokes in *Meadowlands* is inevitably social even if some of those in it are not particularly sociable. It is also distinctly anti-pastoral. The title evokes Arcadia, but it refers as well to the swampy sludge off the New Jersey Turnpike. A marriage partakes of both. A sequence of "Meadowlands" poems inflects the volume with this tension, each a fantasy of pastoral happiness checked by contravening fact. Repeatedly, the volume asks what can be seen without the false lights of romance, with only the plain light of day. The blaze of the forsythia, one of the "emblems of light . . . being / implicitly some earthly / thing transformed" ("Cana"), is brief. Early in the volume the poet asks, "what will we see by, / now that the yellow torches have become / green branches?" ("Cana"). The melancholic speaker may insist on darkness and the endless "*Oi me*" of operatic grief. But that darkness is as untrustworthy, in its way, as the lights of romance. The volume might seem to forfeit imaginative transformation altogether in its commitment to the daylight look of things. Glück's plain style has never been so plain, the understatement so strong a check against emotional excess. But desire does have a place to go in its search for harmony—it moves into music with its temporal transformations. Early in the volume, in "Moonless Night," "a lady weeps at a dark window," a familiar scene. But meanwhile, a neighboring troupe, "The Lights," are "practicing klezmer music," and the last words of "Heart's Desire," the closing poem, bring them back: the passions have been transposed into music: "First *Norma* / then maybe the Lights will play." Between the light of romance and the night of despair there is the consolation of music and, more generally, of art. What the speaker wishes for, she admits, is less the return of lost love than "another poem" ("The Wish").

Humor also creates this tonal balance. *Meadowlands* announces its tragicomic stance in the epigraph: "Let's play choosing music. . . . / Figaro. No. Figaro and Tannhauser." An eyebrow arches even in earlier books, but melancholy and supplication have dominated Glück's work. This is her funniest volume, yet the humor is not trivializing; the somber music retains its claim on the emotions. *Meadowlands* offers a new kind of tragicomedy, less grotesque than Eliot's, less black than Beckett's, more constructive than Berryman's. The incongruity in the opening of "Siren" works to lighten, not darken, the undeveloped disaster plot. Humor here has a corrective force; it measures the limits of the passion and tells us how far to trust it: "I became a criminal when I fell in love. / Before that I was a waitress." This kind of opening shows all its cards and is somehow less manipulative than a more conventional ironic twist at the end, a gesture that so often flaunts the ironic power of the lyric voice—that last resort of the ego, when the imagination or will hits limits. Not that the twists at the ends of Glück's earlier poems aren't wonderfully disarming. In her almost-sonnets they can be especially witty. "Labor Day" (an anti-pastoral from *Firstborn*) begins: "Requiring something lovely on his arm / Took me to Stamford, Connecticut, a quasi-farm." The weekend turns seedy, ending with a rhyme suspended over several lines: "the grass grew limp. . . . / . . . You pimp." But in *Meadowlands* irony is not so much a tactic of revenge and verbal thumbing, a desperate assertion of the speaker's power, as it is a tactic of self-scrutiny and an impetus to revision. The speaker often surprises herself, not just the reader or an apostrophized "you." Glück speaks of this quality of open-mindedness in "Against Sincerity," where she associates it with Keats's negative capability, but more generally with all true art: "At the heart of that work will be a question, a problem. And we will feel, as we read, a sense that the poet was not wed to any one outcome. The poems themselves are like experiments, which the reader is freely invited to recreate in his own mind" (*Proofs & Theories*, 45). In *Meadowlands* questions are often dramatized through humor, or have the effect of humor. For instance, the closing ironies are like moves in a chess match. They are not the poet's possession but rather arise in dialogue, where their motives are exposed. They mark temporary victories or gains in an endless battle with no real victors. If the female wins one round, the male wins the next. Glück plays with the idea that conversation is combat in "The Butterfly," where the net comes down unexpectedly:

> Look, a butterfly. Did you make a wish?
>
> You don't wish on butterflies.
>
> You do so. Did you make one?
>
> Yes.
>
> It doesn't count.

Indeed, sometimes the retort occurs with several poems between, as in "Meadowlands 1" and "Meadowlands 2." Timing is the essence of comedy, but here, added to the timing, is the mimesis of a brooding relationship, in which a trivial quarrel can go on silently for days. To the husband, who idealizes another family's walks in the country and their souvenirs of treasured times, the wife replies:

> Alissa isn't bringing back
> sticks for the house; the sticks
> belong to the dog.

Dialogue is a major defense against the static vocalization of the self. But the humor of the dialogue inheres partly in its failure as communication. The commitment to dialogue as compromise, the last nostalgia of the marriage counselor, is not entertained here. The exchange recalls, rather, Marianne Moore's view of marriage: "that striking grasp of opposites / opposed each to the other, not to unity" ("Marriage"). Much of marriage, it seems, is cross-talk. The poet's role is to listen and play back, not only the self's version of what it hears, but the whole mysterious pattern made by conflicts of will and differences of disposition. The speakers themselves are relentlessly analytical (they have brought therapy into the home, where it becomes a weapon, not an agent of healing). The poet does not add her own analysis of the failed communication (as Beckett and Eliot do, through allusion, stage directions, interpolations), but shows its ritualistic aspect. The willful speakers, while thinking themselves free, seem to be reading from the script of a play they have not written, but which they cannot escape. Whether the talk is of artichokes and furniture, or of Stevens and Flaubert, it is the same conversation.

This predictability does not deprive the speakers of insight. Blindness and insight are necessary partners. Glück's willingness to submit the self to the perspective of the other goes so far in "Void" as to delete the words of the self, which inhabit the white space in an anthology of advice, accusation, retort. These read like stand-up one-liners, yet they evoke the presence of the silent one, whose silence becomes a form of qualified assent. We recognize the speaker's personal investment in this analysis—he is a combatant, not an ally—yet motive does not erase authority:

> You know why you cook? Because
> you like control. A person who cooks is a person who likes
> to create debt.
> . . . .
> Don't think of them as guests, think of them
> as extra chickens. You'd like it.
> If we had more furniture
> you'd have more control.

One suspects that these are not the actual words of a husband, but of a self imagining another's perspective. Glück is interested in a truth finer than actuality, one uncovered by the methods of art.

Glück steps out intermittently from the sequence of songs and dialogues to offer a parable. These parable poems retain the plain style of the volume, yet they offer an outlet, in other ways, for the poetic impulses suppressed, or hidden, elsewhere, especially the impulse to metaphor. While the volume as a whole is blunt, these images are secretive. Like the chorus in a tragedy, parables are removed from the action of the main narrative, in order to comment on it. The form is abstract and impersonal, thus performing another distancing function. Like Jesus's parables, these explain but also obscure their meanings so that they are apparent to the reader but not to the historical characters. We see through a glass, darkly. Through the parables, Glück provides a comprehensive vision and anticipatory truth obscure to the players in the drama. Parables have an ethical function as well as a distancing function—they elucidate the meaning of events, by abstracting and emblematizing them, and by suspending the particulars of the actual world. As we listen, we are caught up in the tale and embrace it as story. The parables, then, introduce a counterpoint to the aggressive analysis the characters offer of each other, always corrupted by their positions in the drama. They locate those perspectives in a larger temporal patterning. Parables are important to the lyric tradition and can be found throughout modern poetry (Frost, Moore, Bishop), but they are more often associated with prose fiction—Dostoevsky, O'Connor, Kafka. In *Meadowlands* they serve both a lyric (transfigurative) and a narrative (transformational) function.

An impersonal and omniscient narrator (the typical narrator of parable) is not necessarily trustworthy, but such a form of narration at least attracts trust. The speaker seems motivated out of a love of truth and clarification, rather than an assertion of desire or will. The parables speak of what is already complete, the event that has happened or whose outcome is not to be altered or controlled, only awaited. As a result, they express a calm in contrast to the passions of the songs. Parables clarify while asserting the underlying mystery in the way things are; hence they often present paradoxes and find truth in enigma. Indeed, they sometimes critique the craving for rational explanation as a form of control. They resist premature closure or judgment. Glück's parables are not transparent, like those of Matthew (the Prodigal Son, the Good Samaritan), but neither are they obscure, like those of Mark, or bizarre, like Kafka's. We feel the guiding presence of the narrator in "Parable of the Swans," a study of narcissism and domestic restlessness. The narrator interrupts the narrative to redirect its interpretation: "But this is not / a little story about the male's / inherent corruption, . . . // It is / a story of guile and innocence. . . ." Both male and female motives are examined, but finally the narration refuses to take sides, withdrawing into observation and detached recounting: "On the muddy water / they bickered awhile, in the fading light, / until the bickering grew / slowly abstract, becoming / part of their song / after a little while." Especially early in the volume, the parables tend to present a tension between the omniscience of the speaker, who knows the outcome, and the limited vision of the characters it fastens on.

In "Parable of the Hostages," for instance, Glück achieves this tension through the use of the present tense and the interrogative mood. The internal questioning of the characters yields to the narrative questioning. An "ah" of ironic but also ethical wisdom (a wisdom without agency that can be heard in "ah's" through-out this volume) marks the gap in knowledge characteristic of tragedy:

> what if war
> is just a male version of dressing up,
> a game devised to avoid
> profound spiritual questions? Ah,
> but it wasn't only the war. The world had begun
> calling them, an opera beginning with the war's
> loud chords and ending with the floating aria of the sirens.
> . . . .
> how could the Greeks know
> they were hostage already: who once
> delays the journey is
> already enthralled; how could they know
> that of their small number
> some would be held forever by the dreams of pleasure,
> some by sleep, some by music?

The first parable, "The Parable of the King," reinforces the theme of the limits of power and knowledge. The characters in *Meadowlands* think they choose their destinies. The parable presents a different view. It is an appropriate way to introduce a sequence that maps a progress from expectation to conclusion:

> The great king looking ahead
> saw not fate but simply
> dawn glittering over
> the unknown island. . . .

The poem ends with a retrospective view, such as Yeats employed in "Leda and the Swan":

                    Whatever
it was ahead, why did it have to be
so blinding? Who could have known
that wasn't the usual sun
but flames rising over a world
about to become extinct?

One feels, throughout the narration, a great pity for the king, who enters his fate so helplessly, thinking it is his creation. Hubris is the error these parables so often correct.

"Parable of the Trellis," too, moves from the simple language of fact to the ambiguities of interpretation. Glück has studied the genre carefully and knows its idiom. Like so many parables, this one begins with a short, descriptive sentence to initiate a story: "A clematis grew at the foot of a great trellis." But again, the moral of this simple tale is full of paradox, and the understanding shifts as the poem proceeds. Here, in the middle of the poem, a false path is offered and withdrawn. The ruse of domestic pastoral is exposed. Meadowlands are full of mind-traps, "a quiet evening" surrounded by a "life-threatening forest." As "Parable of the Trellis" proceeds, it examines this very impulse to "ruse," to dream of an ideal. The allegorical meanings are hidden, in parable fashion, but clearly the vine has something to do with human desire, which binds itself to structure and foundation—domestic arrangements, marriage, reality—in order to realize its dream:

                Remember, to the vine, the trellis
                was never an image of confinement:
                this is not
                diminishment or tragedy.

                The vine has a dream of light:
                what is life in the dirt
                with its dark freedoms
                compared to supported ascent?

                And for a time,
                every summer we could see the vine
                relive this decision, thus
                obscuring the wood, structure
                beautiful in itself, like
                a harbor or willow tree.

The final ambiguity—is marriage a place of return or of loss and mourning?—characterizes the modern parable's resistance to moral tags, its way of being in uncertainties and enigmas, which is a kind of wisdom.

Most of the parables in *Meadowlands* are also fables, which contributes to their humor. Human behavior, understood in terms of plants and animals, is less a matter of will than of instinct. "Parable of the Swans" is a parody of self-love and disdain for the muck of ordinary life. The swans swim on the lake, admiring themselves in "the attentive water" and occasionally "administering to the beloved other" in their sequestered space, until "they hit slimy water . . . simultaneously, / the true purpose of his neck's / flexible design revealed itself. So much . . . / he's missed!" The arch tone here could again be Marianne Moore, but where her animals tend to exemplify values, Glück's affront our narcissism. Since we have Circe, we naturally have pigs here, but that's not her fault: "I never turned anyone into a pig. / Some people are pigs; I make them/look like pigs" ("Circe's Power"). Irony, rather than paradox, is the emotional outcome in the fables. Faithful Penelope has a dark side that would send her lover to hell before she would forgive him: "perhaps I have / the soul of a reptile, after all," she says to the serpent, in a poem ironically entitled "The Rock." The cat who creeps in and out of the volume is a figure for the petulant inner life. In "Parable of the Beast" the domestic pet sinks "its teeth" into "the flesh of another animal," the dead bird (of the idealizing spirit?) indecorously imported into the kitchen.

Not all the fables are humorous, however. In some the irony is tragic, recalling Oscar Wilde's fairy tales more than Aesop's fables. "Parable of the Dove" tells a story of the sacrificial spirit, investing itself in human feeling rather than metaphysical flight. It is the most self-referential of the parables:

> the world drew back; the mutant
> fell from love
> as from the cherry branch,
> it fell stained with the bloody
> fruit of the tree.
>
> So it is true after all, not merely
> a rule of art:
> change your form and you change your nature.
> And time does this to us.

Parable, whether in prose or poetry, is a narrative art; its material is time. And time is one of the great disrupters of self-absorption, an impingement on the steady flow of desire toward any object, especially when that object is the self. The myth of Narcissus, Glück reminds us in "American Narcissism," is "all psychology, no narrative. As a static image, it encourages projections of the kind narrative limits or interrupts." Narrative forces movement out toward the world and implies change, whereas the pure lyric never ends, only recycles.[3] *Meadowlands* opens up those narrative limits and interruptions, shows the world as more than a stimulus for the self's passive response, and shows the self as agent as well as receptor. And of course Ovid's story is a parable too—a narrative of tragic constriction in the homage to the self. The closures of narrative work against iconic repetition and stasis. The lyric's investment in the moment as an eternity, or rather, its elegiac sense of the present (every poem is an epitaph), gives us the figure at the beginning of "Moonless Night." There is no outer world for the weeping woman, but other life does go on for the reader to see. Glück will not ask us, as so many lyric poets do, to dwell on this fixed image forever. But nor is she especially concerned, as the strictly narrative artist must be, with conclusion. Instead, she looks ahead, abandoning absorption for the different satisfaction of change:

> On the other side, there could be anything,
> all the joy in the world, the stars fading,
> the streetlight becoming a bus stop.

This is not to suggest that Glück has abandoned lyric's meditative, memorializing purpose, its defiant relation to time. In some way narrative and lyric are embodied in the figures of Penelope and Odysseus, whose marriage may not last, but whose union produces a particular kind of music, recursive, yet temporally patterned. For Odysseus "time / begins now, in which he hears again / that pulse which is the narrative / sea" ("Odysseus' Decision"). Penelope's pulse is set to a different repetition, the weaving and unweaving of the moment, which is the essence of the recursive lyric form. Penelope knows that travel is always a craving to return, a "nostos" which can never be satisfied, but to which poetry is dedicated: "We look at the world once, in childhood / The rest is memory" ("Nostos"), fixed in immutable image. It is one of the many strengths of *Meadowlands* that it gives voice to both of these irrefutable truths.

NOTES

1. *Firstborn* is included in *The First Four Books of Poems.*
2. *Threepenny Review* 72 (winter 1998): 5–7.
3. Glück's fascination with the use of narrative in lyric is evident in her essay "Story Tellers," about Robert Pinsky and Stephen Dobyns. Her emphasis there is on the introduction of cause-and-effect patterning into the stillness of the lyric. See *American Poetry Review* 26 (July–August 1997): 9–12.

Splendor and Mistrust

I.

Most poets who are good at the hieratic like the hieratic. Louise Glück is one of the exceptions.

By "the hieratic" I mean the sense that, in moments of intense emotion, life becomes charged and even a little stylized; everything has meaning, a door seems to open onto a higher realm. By "like" I mean . . .

But let's look at a poem, "The Fear of Love":

> That body lying beside me like obedient stone—
> once its eyes seemed to be opening,
> we could have spoken.
>
> At that time it was winter already.
> By day the sun rose in its helmet of fire
> and at night also, mirrored in the moon.
>
> Its light passed over us freely,
> as though we had lain down
> in order to leave no shadows,
> only these two shallow dents in the snow.
> And the past, as always, stretched before us,
> still, complex, impenetrable.
>
> How long did we lie there
> as, arm in arm in their cloaks of feathers,
> the gods walked down
> from the mountain we built for them?

I don't know any other poem that so conveys the otherworldliness in sexual passion, yet makes it seem eerie, spooky even, not altogether desirable. Of the passion, and its quality of a visitation, animal and supernatural, there can be no doubt—

> . . . arm in arm in their cloaks of feathers,
> the gods walked down
> from the mountain we built for them

Yet the season is winter, not summer, the bed like a snowfield. To lie down in snow, voluntarily, is to freeze to death; to "leave no shadows" is perhaps to lose one's identity. The oxymoron "obedient stone" hints at two of our deepest, most tyrannous wishes about love—that it should be monumental, and yet fit our every whim—but also suggests the stillness of a corpse. Even the timelessness of passion becomes uncanny, the mirroring moon indistinguishable from the armed, helmeted sun. Perhaps the source of uncanniness lies in the Freudian sense that love is repetition—that the "still," unchangeable "past," not the future, "stretched before us." But if so, one feels the poem would almost rather have focused on that grim insight, and so remained in the realm of the "spoken," than have suffered its wordless urgencies directly.

Louise Glück has said, in her essay "The Dreamer and the Watcher," that she often writes poems backward, beginning with the abstract insight she wants to demonstrate:

> Other imaginations begin, I believe, in the actual, in the world, in some concrete thing which examination endows with significance. . . . My own work begins at the opposite end, at the end, literally, at illumination, which has then to be traced back to some source in the world. This method, when it succeeds, makes a thing that seems irrefutable. Its failure is felt as portentousness. (*Proofs & Theories,* 101)

One can bet that the concluding "illumination" is often a grim one, that has to be "irrefutable" because the reader might want to refute it. The end of "Palais des Arts," a poem about "Love long dormant showing itself," is surely a prime example:

> She can't touch his arm in innocence again.
> They have to give that up and begin
> as male and female, thrust and ache.

Knowing how much most readers (except perhaps lesbian separatists, of whom Glück is definitely not one) will hate this definition of the genders, the body of the poem seems to say, *look here,* as it points to the two friends-become-lovers, who seem "paralyzed," unable to speak, because of the new weight each action has taken on. The sense that life is more organized, aesthetically, at moments of passion becomes a topic almost of satire, as this poem reuses the central trope of "The Fear of Love": the "gods," now museum caryatids, are "large" and "expected," and their position behind columns allows the speaker to say they are "caged really." The pseudo-classicism of museum décor becomes a vehicle for protesting the rigidity, the reduction to an archetype or a role, that can come with intense feeling. The poem prefers friendship to love, as "The Fear of Love" prefers the "spoken" to the wordless. Yet it cannot quite avoid, though it can satirize, the connection of passion not only to the aesthetic, but to Glück's particular ideal of severity—"restraint so passionate / implies possession."

Glück's stance seems a protest against the overwhelming processes of life itself, its power to change us against our will; a "disposition not to acquiesce," she writes in "The Dreamer and the Watcher," "will always inform my work: an aspect of character" (*Proofs & Theories,* 101). At best, as in the poem uncharacteristically titled "Happiness," process is "the burning wheel" which, for once, "passes gently over us." The paradox that to accept life is also to accept death is never far from Glück's mind. In "Celestial Music," she writes, "I'm always moved by weakness, by disaster, always eager to oppose vitality," as if the two statements obviously go together. In the essay quoted above, she also says that her "poems . . . reserve their love for what doesn't exist." This might sound like a religious sentiment; but in the poems what are ordinarily thought of as experiences of the sacred inspire the same vehement distrust that *eros* does, perhaps because they too require some acceptance of process. In "Celestial Music," the speaker finds a friend's religious belief baffling, because it involves the ability to surrender to life, to "watch, to let events play out / according to nature," and still maintain an attitude of acceptance: "when you love the world you hear celestial music." To the speaker, such a vision—like *eros,* with which it remains curiously intertwined—can only be a trap:

> look up, she says. When I look up, nothing.
> Only clouds, snow, a white business in the trees
> like brides leaping to a great height—
> Then I'm afraid for her; I see her
> caught in a net deliberately cast over the earth—

Robert Hass comments on the "startling" metaphorical splendor given, once again, to what is rejected: "the snow in the branches, which is always a little like blossoms, as a bride caught there. It is a sort of Kore myth transposed upward, a gnostic retelling in which the love of life, the moment of its blossoming and ceremony, traps us." (He goes on to make the intriguing suggestion that the cynicism, however deeply felt, has social and familial overtones: "The phrase that summarizes both nature and desire so dismissively, the 'white business in the trees,' seems to come out of the particular idiom of a family, of a time and a place.")[1]

It's tempting simply to say that the friend's stance in the poem is religious, that Glück's is skeptical. But a skeptic does not imagine a malevolent cosmos "deliberately" casting nets. It might be more accurate to say that while the friend's acceptance is Christian or Buddhist, Glück's stance is not only "gnostic" but—like the family idiom—Jewish. It is the voice of David, Jeremiah, or Job arguing personally and reproachfully, as one can argue with a Lord who has a Chosen People, who writes (or does not write) each person's name in the Book of Life once a year. Glück gives this voice free rein in the "Matins" and "Vespers" sections of her most ambitious book on religious topics, *The Wild Iris:*

> You must see
> it is useless to us, this silence that promotes belief
> you must be all things, the foxglove and the hawthorn
>   tree,
> the vulnerable rose and tough daisy—we are left to think
> you couldn't possibly exist.

(Perhaps she gives this voice too free rein; this is the one book of Glück's since *Firstborn* that occasionally sounds querulous to me, or sentimental.) In any case, the Hebrew God (whose unutterable name the young Robert Lowell memorably rendered "IS") can only reply, as he replies to Job, in the changes of the weather—that is to say, as Fate. And what He says is always the same: *my ways are not as your ways:*

> After all things occurred to me,
> the void occurred to me.
>
> There is a limit
> to the pleasure I had in form—

I am not like you in this,
I have no release in another body, . . .
　　　　　　　　　　　—"End of Summer"

But, returning to "Celestial Music," I am particularly moved by
the paradoxical, category-breaking discovery the speaker makes at
the end: that the friend's religious acceptance and her own resistance
are not as far apart as they first appeared. Seeing her friend "dra[w]
a circle in the dirt" around the dying caterpillar, the speaker understands that the same impulse to stand outside life, to find the still
point from which one can make an "irrefutable" statement, can un-
derlie mystical assent as well as unflinching realism:

> She's always trying to make something whole, something
> 　　　　beautiful, an image
> capable of life apart from her.

Both characters, in truth, are equally "at ease with death, with solitude," perhaps because both participate in the aesthetic impulse.
That impulse, Glück now understands, whether it takes the form of
"celestial music" or grim, decisive statement, always partakes of the
hieratic, the desire to hold "the composition / fixed." But by the
same token, even in the mystic, it "oppose[s] vitality":

> The love of form is a love of endings.

Joanne Feit Diehl has argued that the great American women
poets have all been averse to the Sublime, as Emerson defined it:
"abandonment to the nature of things . . . suffering the ethereal
tides to roll and circulate through him."[2] Women poets, Diehl
writes, are less assured that they have the "capacity to survive such
an upheaval intact," partly because both its likely sources, in psychoanalytic terms—"the image of patriarchal authority . . . or . . . a
feminine image, Mother Nature who weds as she nurtures her
son"—are more problematic for them than for men (2–3). Hence,
the only way they could manifest the energy of the Sublime, yet
preserve the integrity of their own perspective, was in the very ve-
hemence of their resistance to it: "Confrontation with an authoritative natural or intellectual spirit appears in Dickinson's poems as
a conflict between a defensive subject and—an 'essential adversary'" (27). Thus the various skepticisms and rebarbativenesses not
only of Dickinson but of Moore, Bishop, Plath. The alternative

stance—that of the enthralled erotic votary—was left to the de-spised "poetesses," Wylie, Millay.

Glück belongs to a different poetic generation, one that seems to refute Diehl's prediction that the American woman poet "will be forced either to redefine her sexuality or to evade it" (139). (Brenda Hillman and Jorie Graham also come to mind.) These poets seem no more afraid of explicit heterosexual *eros* than the great Russians—Akhmatova, Tsvetayeva–were. Yet a case could be made that Glück's distrust of "the nature of things" is still gendered, still in some way a refusal of an invasive male presence, as well as of easy male affirma-tions. To kiss is to be deprived of speech, "the man's mouth / sealing my mouth"—an idea Glück likes enough that she uses it twice, in "Mock Orange" and in the "Grandmother" section of "Dedication to Hunger." To believe in God is to feel the world being created around one by an alien intruder, a "gold eye / projecting flowers on the landscape," perhaps "a monster" ("Lamentations"). Experiences of the religious sublime are, as we have seen throughout, often con-flated with heterosexual love. So Glück's severe apartness can be seen as a refusal of male influence; in "Dedication to Hunger" it is com-pared to the anorexia that "begins . . . in certain female children":

> I felt
> what I feel now, aligning these words—
> it is the same need to perfect,
> of which death is the mere byproduct.

The atmosphere of "Celestial Music," too, is one of women whose creative individuality emerges because they can do without men, "at ease with death, with *solitude*" (italics mine). Perhaps, for Glück, female creativity must gravitate toward this version of "easeful death," for fear of the opposite death of being overwhelmed in the act of acceptance. In any case, Glück clearly belongs in Diehl's ge-nealogy in this largest sense: her way of manifesting splendor, emo-tional and linguistic, in the act of defending against it is the very essence of the Counter-Sublime.

II.

I witnessed something curious at a reading in Berkeley in 1990, just after *Ararat* was published. As Glück read lines like

> My mother's an expert in one thing:
> sending people she loves into the other world.

or

> No one could write a novel about this family;
> too many similar characters. Besides, they're all women;
> there was only one hero.

waves of chuckles spread over the audience. Then, as the reading continued, the laughter stopped. Something—Glück's somber monotone, the unremitting focus on death—had made the audience's spontaneous reaction feel inappropriate. Criticism, too, has been slow to acknowledge how often, and how brilliantly, the later Glück is a comic poet. And yet, to me, there is nothing surprising in this development. One cannot remain forever in the posture of disappointment or protest against "vitality." To stand outside everyone else's modes of hope and comfort, yet express more than childlike stubbornness, is to become a satirist: Swift's stance, not Shelley's.

Yet good satire has a way, finally, of not just being about other people. The self, too, becomes the target. The divorce poems in *Meadowlands,* written as dialogue, are such a delight not only because they capture, so perfectly, the unkindnesses only people who know each other intimately are capable of, but because they also feel like a dialogue between the two forces that have warred in Glück's poetry from early on. In "Meadowlands I," what I'll call Voice A begins the song of "vitality," presenting its unstoppable belief that if *we* do not feel in harmony with our lives, someone else, somewhere, does:[3]

> I wish we went on walks
> like Steve and Kathy; then
> we'd be happy. You can even see it
> in the dog.

Voice B comes back not only with "fact," as Frost would say, but with what we have come to recognize as Glück's characteristic values:

> We don't have a dog.
> We have a hostile cat.

> I think Sam's
> intelligent; he
> resents being a pet.
>
> Why is it always family with you?
> Can't we ever be two adults?

Even in an animal, to be "intelligent" is to "resent" roles, especially those that offer nurturance in exchange for freedom; "adults" are above all such womb-like, "family" nostalgias.

But to A, self-deception is not the horror it is to B. (We remember, from "The Dreamer and the Watcher," Glück's understanding of the Eros and Psyche myth: "Psyche leaning over Eros stood for the human compulsion to see, to know, for the rejection of whatever comfort derives from deception" [*Proofs & Theories,* 102]). To A, illusion can be the lovable, comic fault that—because we all share it—restores us to the whole. Again, animals are the example:

> Look how happy Captain is, how
> at peace in the world. Don't you love
> how he sits on the lawn, staring up at the birds? He thinks
> because he's white they can't see him.

But the ultimate poignancy of this poem is that B cannot quite do without A, or the ideals he would like them to embody. She offers this rather pathetic compromise:

> If we don't expect
> Sam to follow, couldn't we
> take him along?

Yet even here, as A's earlier idyll is subtly coercive ("Don't you love . . ."), B does not forego the power politics of marriage: "You could hold him."

In my experience, the farther I read in this book, the more I love, and wince at, these two voices: they are such seasoned, and convincing, marital warriors. But my sense remains that they are simultaneously inner voices: that A is there to include more hope, more idealism than Glück has shown previously, and at the same time to be more probing about the egotism, the secondary gain, involved in the wish "not to acquiesce." There are moments when B, speaking to herself, sounds very much like A, as in "Rainy Morning":

Look at John, out in the world,
running even on a miserable day
like today. Your
staying dry is like the cat's pathetic
preference for hunting dead birds: completely

consistent with your tame spiritual themes,
autumn, loss, darkness, etc.

We can all write about suffering
with our eyes closed. You should show people
more of yourself; show them your clandestine
passion for red meat.

(The "passion for red meat" foreshadows A's devastating comment that "the only time you're totally happy / is when you cut up a chicken," and that, to be more "gregarious," B might "[not] think of them as guests, think of them / as extra chickens.")

By the end of the book, there seems to me a kind of dialectical synthesis, even a reversal, of the two voices. And now, paradoxically, she is the one voicing a vision of imagined perfection, while A has taken on the role of rationalist and critic. In the last poem in the book, "Heart's Desire," B plans a party, implicitly to celebrate their divorce:

I want to do two things:
I want to order meat from Lobel's
and I want to have a party.

You hate parties. You hate
any group bigger than four.

If I hate it
I'll go upstairs. Also
I'm only inviting people who can cook.
Good cooks and all my old lovers.
Maybe even your ex-girlfriends, except
the exhibitionists.

If I were you,
I'd start with the meat order.

But the party is more than a chance to even scores, or to take the risk involved in extending the possibilities of the self ("If I hate it /

I'll go upstairs"). It is a chance, finally, to envision a world in which everyone is "happy":

> When you look into people's faces
> you'll see how happy they are
> . . . .
>
> It will be spring again; all
> the tulips will be opening.

Just *how* extraordinary a party this is, is conveyed by A's chilling rejoinder:

> The point isn't whether or not
> the guests are happy.
>
> The point is whether or not
> they're dead.

But B ignores this objection as she soars into her concluding aria:

> Trust me: no one's
> going to be hurt again.
> For one night, affection
> will triumph over passion. The passion
> will all be in the music.
>
> If you can hear the music
> you can imagine the party.
> I have it all planned: first
> violent love, then
> sweetness. First *Norma*
> then maybe the Lights will play.

(We see just how inclusive this ending is when we remember that "the Lights" are the people A envied for bringing the dog on walks, the people whose "klezmer music" provoked B's dour remark, "A good night: the clarinet is in tune.")

    This party is, I think, the one we all want art to give—the least blind, most livable and intriguing of our human visions of paradise; the one least reducible to a defense against death. The imagination's sense of fullness reigns in the enveloping music; yet the living world, in its unpredictability, is invited. There is forgiveness, within the limits of human capacity (the Lights may be included; "the exhibitionists" are not). Opposites are reconciled, the dead and the living, and even more important, perhaps, for Glück, "passion" and "affection." For "passion," we can now see, has always been double-edged in her work, so fiercely resisted because it is experienced as so compelling, so—if I may return to the word—hieratic. It stands in the way of truth, as in her retelling of the Eros and Psyche story; but both stand in the way of the familial affections, of acceptance of people as they are.

Perhaps art, for all of us, is the place where we can momentarily stand outside those contradictions that seem most tyrannous in our private versions of "reality." "Heart's Desire" is Glück's vision of that between-place, the peculiar version dictated by the urgencies of her character. Because "passion" has been absorbed by the medium itself—it "will all be in the music"—people can at last be seen clearly and at the same time be seen as "happy," seen, even, with "sweetness." It this the Sublime? It is and it isn't, as so many moments in great poetry are and are not. The "ethereal tides" do "roll and circulate through," as Emerson said, but the poet's is the hand on the phonograph needle; and the integrity of the quieter, harsher voice, that integrity which, Diehl argues, American women poets have sacrificed so much to preserve, is never quite drowned out.

NOTES

1. Robert Hass, "Families and Prisons," *Michigan Quarterly Review* 30 (fall 1991): 572.

2. See Joanne Feit Diehl, *Women Poets and the American Sublime* (Bloomington: Indiana University Press, 1990) 1. Subsequent references will appear in the text.

3. I use the term "Voice A" to refer to the sections beginning at the left margin and "Voice B" to refer to the indented sections. Sometimes, though, a single-voiced poem, beginning at the left margin, sounds to me like Voice B in the dialogue poems, and I have so designated it.

STEPHEN BURT

"The Dark Garage with the Garbage"

Louise Glück's Structures

Psychologists call it depressive realism: the notion, still debated in a raft of experiments, is that some depressed people prove especially good at predicting what they and others will do, because their divorce from their own hopes makes them able to see, and willing to describe, facts and emotions the rest of us block or deny.[1] Depressive realism is a secret strength of Louise Glück's work: it connects Glück's stark and straitened tones to the insights her poems contain. Her distance from those she describes (herself included) lets her see them with cold acuteness; coming to love a Glück poem means coming to empathize with the bitter self-consciousness her skeletal arrangements reflect. In particular, understanding her depressive realism means understanding the ways in which her poems use endings. A successful Glück poem demonstrates its depressive realism by drawing unwelcome conclusions, potential endings, not once but many times before it concludes; Glück's transitional volume *Meadowlands* both demonstrates and complicates her depressive-realist orientation, along with the tactics of multiple endings that orientation has entailed.

Glück wrote, accurately, in *Proofs & Theories,* "My work has always been strongly marked by a disregard for the circumstantial, except insofar as it could be transformed into paradigm" (100–101). Helen Vendler, in *The Music of What Happens,* explains that Glück's poetry "turns away from specific details and observations . . . to an abstract plane"; her poems go in fear of description, speeding from anecdotes, myths, or scenes straight to their general meanings—meanings other poets might embroider or evade.[2] Glück's tendencies to strip and simplify both the events she depicts and the language in

---

An earlier version appeared in *PN Review* 125 (1999). Thanks to Michael Schmidt and Carcanet Press for allowing it to be reprinted here.

which she depicts them can come across both as a refusal of fanciful hopes, and as a way to dignify painful experience: as Maggie Tulliver puts it in *The Mill on the Floss,* "If we use common words on a great occasion, they are the more striking, because they are felt at once to have a particular meaning, like old banners or everyday clothes hung up in a sacred place."[3]

Glück's best work from the 1970s and 1980s had precisely this effect, surprising us with the persistent disjunction between its common words and its exceptional states of feeling. Half the force of "Mock Orange," from *The Triumph of Achilles,* springs from its shocking prose meaning, and half from the carefully laid-out barrenness of its terms:[4]

> It is not the moon, I tell you.
> It is these flowers
> lighting the yard.
>
> I hate them.
> I hate them as I hate sex,
> the man's mouth
> sealing my mouth, the man's
> paralyzing body—
>
> and the cry that always escapes,
> the low, humiliating
> premise of union—

The denuded language can lead readers to think such lines artless, even as they are shocked and moved by them. There is, of course, art here, and not only in the rhythms—"premise" replaces the expected "promise," and the repeated one-syllable words mime Glück's repeated (literally "anticlimactic") frustrations.[5] But the psychological extremity makes the art part difficult for new readers to see. By ruling out certain axes of variation—confining herself to a narrow palette of diction, for example—Glück's depressive style makes other kinds of aesthetic choices (chiefly structural and grammatical) bear exceptional weight.

Often these choices emphasize ideas of closure. "The love of form is a love of endings," Glück concludes two books earlier, in *Ararat* ("Celestial Music"). An earlier poem in *The Triumph of Achilles* explains that the sturdy elm "will make no forms but twisted forms" ("Elms"): Glück's own forms twist and double back so as to emphasize their endings. Her poems display often—sometimes from beginning to end—several features Barbara Herrnstein Smith, in her well-known study of "how poems end," associates with closure, among them an "authority of unqualified assertion" (with its resulting "tone of authority"), a "settled finality" appropriate to "apparently self-evident truth," and a focus on "terminal events" (e.g., "death, night, autumn and farewells").[6] Glück's works thus seem to struggle, as Glück has said that she herself struggles, against an unusually strong impetus toward closure; their sense of cold finality comes in part from the ways they seem always ready to stop. Glück's sequences of abrupt breaks, near-endings, and general statements lead at last to unshakably final termini, like this one from *The Triumph of Achilles:* "So it was settled: I could have a childhood there. / Which came to mean being always alone" ("Marathon").

One of Glück's signature structures is that of a whole poem built from potential endings, from lines and sentences most of which might have terminated the poem. (We can think of such structures as the resultants when two of Glück's most powerful drives interact: the impulse toward closure and the desire for self-remaking.) This way of making a poem go on implies that the poem will terminate at whatever truth we least want to hear, or have the most invested in evading: "Spring Snow," from *The Wild Iris,* done with images, concludes:

> You can close your eyes now.
> I have heard your cries, and cries before yours,
> and the demand behind them.
> I have shown you what you want:
> not belief, but capitulation
> to authority, which depends on violence.

"Now" and "them" sound like avoided endings, sites where Glück decides she must say more. Glück's desire to correct herself, and to make whole poems out of gestures of ending, leads her to conceive of other poems as sequences of negations. One of the prayerlike "Matins" poems from *The Wild Iris* has the explicit logical structure of *if not X, then Y; if not Y, at least Z; if not even Z, then at least A:*

> Father,
> as agent of my solitude, alleviate
> at least my guilt; lift

the stigma of isolation, unless
it is your plan to make me
sound forever again, as I was
sound and whole in my mistaken childhood,
or if not then, under the light weight
of my mother's heart, or if not then,
in dream, first
being that would never die.

Almost every one of Glück's best poems gives a new meaning and a new incarnation to some such device of successive closure. To love *her* forms, in particular, is to love endings.

Glück's attraction to summaries, conclusions, decisions, makes up part of her depressive style—one might even say of "depressive style" generally. In an important poem from *The Wild Iris* (the second in the book, and the first not spoken by a flower) Glück classifies herself matter-of-factly as a "depressive" who makes the characteristic "error of depressives," identifying with wholes rather than parts ("Matins"). (The essayist Nancy Mairs writes similarly of her own depressive, self-claustrating tastes: "I love closure. . . . I like to tie off the tale with some statement that sounds as though nothing further could be said" [*Plaintext,* 91]). Glück's recent insistence that she is "drawn to the unfinished, to sentences that falter," and "dislike[s] poems that feel too complete" seems less descriptive than aspirational.[7] Elsewhere Glück implies that her much-emphasized self-breakings and self-transformations arise as healthy reactions to what would otherwise be her destructive "dependency or addiction" to self-punishment and self-control.[8]

Glück's (depressive) drive to repudiate, revise, and draw new conclusions from old operates not only within her poems, but from one book to the next. Every one of her books of poetry, Glück declares, "has culminated in a conscious diagnostic act, a swearing-off" (*Proofs & Theories,* 17). Drawn to Glück's prose, and encouraged by the nature of book reviewing to consider how each book reacts to the one before, Glück's critics have concentrated on the ways Glück varies from book to book, rather than on her range from poem to poem. Her attempts to remake herself from book to book are nowhere more obvious than in her seventh book, *Meadowlands.* Seeing how *Meadowlands* responds to Glück's earlier work, we can also see what rhythmic, grammatical, and structural choices still propel her poems, and still distinguish them from one another.

Each of Glück's mature books imped its wing on a body of myth: *The Triumph of Achilles* used Ovid and the *Iliad, Ararat* cited the Book of Genesis, and *The Wild Iris* took off from a bevy of floral legends. The backdrop for *Meadowlands* is the *Odyssey,* whose vengeful leave-takings and homecomings shadow the breakup of Glück's marriage; she writes, again, out of her interpersonal life, addressing conjunctions between myths and pictures and her own behavior. Her best new poems there sound like her best old ones, with the same astringent perceptiveness: who else would call her soul "little perpetually undressed one," or write, about pairs of swans, that "their fame as lovers stems / chiefly from narcissism, which leaves / so little leisure for / more general cruising" ("The Parable of the Swans")? But her oddest new poems are departures indeed from the portentous condensations and insights of *The Wild Iris;* they are bits of almost kitchen-sink realist dialogue between the speaker and her ex-husband, or the speaker and their neighbors. "Ceremony" and its kin violate every principle of exclusion Glück earlier set herself:

> Living with you is like living
> at boarding school:
> chicken Monday, fish Tuesday,
> . . . .
>
> We have fish Tuesday
> because it's fresh Tuesday. If I could drive
> we could have it different days.

Such notated trivia depend for their effects on our recognizing what they have *replaced,* what kind of conclusive seriousness her cadences "ought" to contain and do not: encountering the household detritus of the dialogue poems, a reader used to the Glück of "Mock Orange" or of *Ararat* may feel like a child, afraid of ghosts and noises, who shines a flashlight into a closet only to find hockey sticks, pillows, old shoes.

As perversely accomplished as the ruminations on the Giants are, the final power of *Meadowlands* comes mostly from the poems that can stand on their own, those which display (like "Mock Orange") "depressive" style and successive closures. One such poem is "Cana":

What can I tell you that you don't know
that will make you tremble again?

Forsythia
by the roadside, by
wet rocks, on the embankments
underplanted with hyacinth—

For ten years I was happy.
You were there; in a sense,
you were always with me, the house, the garden
constantly lit,
not with light as we have in the sky
but with those emblems of light
which are more powerful, being
implicitly some earthly
thing transformed—

And all of it vanished,
reabsorbed into impassive process. Then
what will we see by,
now that the yellow torches have become
green branches?

Glück's characteristic succession of closures here appears first in-
verted, as a series of three beginnings, and then as three retrospects,
each of which covers a different time frame: the distant past, the recent past, and the moment just before this one, when flowers gave
way to leaves. Jesus turned water into wine for the wedding at Cana
when his host's supply ran out: Glück's title suggests that only a
miracle could replenish her marriage, or make it flower again.

The poem finds its final starting point in its first complete in-
dicative sentence: "For ten years I was happy." Now that she has
returned to her (normal) *un*happiness, she sees the year as a set
of oppositions: spring, marriage, home, containment, youth, the
metaphorical ("emblems"), "yellow torches" (flowers), as against
summer, divorce, roads, ongoingness, maturity, the literal, and
"green branches" (leaves). Glück's final sentence unites her gram-
matically with her ex-husband, in the pronoun "we," for the first
time: "I" and "you" were not very similar—no more so than gardens are like constellations—but in their lasting separateness the

poet and her former husband are (ironically) at last as alike as two weeds. Breaking a line on "then" gives the word two meanings, the first temporal—"what will happen to us *next?*"—and the second causative—*if* the constellations are gone and the luminous roadside flowers are gone, *then* what will illuminate our separate lives?

Another way to put *that* question is to ask what psychological poets should do once they have exhausted their best personal material. Should they spy on other people? Should they generate new drama in their own lives? Or should they delve for new conceptions of poetry, ones which won't depend on revealing deep secrets? Before *Meadowlands* Glück assumed that we prove we are real by exposing our worst sides: "Love in Moonlight" (from *The Wild Iris*) equates "despair" with authenticity:

> Sometimes a man or woman forces his despair
> on another person, which is called
> baring the heart, alternatively, baring the soul—
> meaning for this moment they acquired souls—

By contrast, "Moonless Night" (along with several other poems in *Meadowlands)* tries to reject the idea that we are ever identical with our troubles, or, at least, that poems should expose those troubles:

> A lady weeps at a dark window.
> Must we say what it is? Can't we simply say
> a personal matter? It's early summer;
> next door, the Lights are practising klezmer music.
> A good night: the clarinet is in tune.
>
> As for the lady—she's going to wait forever;
> there's no point in watching longer.
> After awhile, the streetlight goes out.
>
> But is waiting forever
> always the answer? Nothing
> is always the answer; the answer
> depends on the story.
>
> Such a mistake to want
> clarity above all things. What's

a single night, especially
one like this, now so close to ending?
On the other side, there could be anything,
all the joy in the world, the stars fading,
the streetlight becoming a bus stop.

Local, lively, and free of grand ambitions, klezmer (the music of
Eastern European Jews, now being revived in America) is the opposite of the opera ("Figaro" and "Tannhauser") Glück namechecks
elsewhere. The set of potential endings in "Moonless Night" op-
poses two kinds of temporal succession: the action of narrative
(where events advance a "story" about people) and the passage of
time in nature (where the sun simply rises and sets, without sus-
pense, climax, or "personal matter"). The neighbors' instrumental
music has no tragedy, no plot of any kind, and the poet wishes to
learn from the Lights how to be satisfied with plotlessness.[9]

One way—the only way, for a poet of Glück's compressing, organizing temperament—is to arrange one's percepts and thoughts
into tight schemes that rule out plot: to make poems that look less
like operas or stories than like instrumental music. Restricted to
weak verbs ("is," "want," "become," "depend"), the end of the poem
relies on its rhythms, alighting on the self-descriptive "stop" as the
sun comes up. The active verbs drop out exactly when the Lights,
and the lady, have vanished: from there to the close we hear, and
"see," only the speaker, whose paralysis the poem displays. The poet
doesn't know what's on the "other side," doesn't know *how* to enjoy
a bus stop, though she knows other people can: the point, the
pathos, of the poem is that she tries and fails. Dawn ends the poem
the evening began: Glück, trying hard to like the world, has stayed
up all night.

The cold tones, the "manner . . . of fated recognition" (as Vendler
puts it in *The Music of What Happens* [248]) which Glück developed
early on, are the tones and manners she takes to extremes in *Ararat,*
a book Calvin Bedient describes as "articulated depression."[10] By
the time of *The Wild Iris* and (more so) of *Meadowlands,* these tones
have become conscious tools, the most important among the several instruments for which Glück scores her poems. "Moonless
Night" keeps up one numbed tone almost throughout, as if Glück
were staring her listener down; another, faster-paced new species of
Glück poem veers wildly between lush, sub-Rilkean lyricism and
theatrical taunting or hectoring. Either alone would sink a poem,

but the combination—while it does sink a few—can make for a new kind of success, like "Midnight," from *Meadowlands:*

> Speak to me, aching heart: what
> ridiculous errand are you inventing for yourself
> weeping in the dark garage
> with your sack of garbage: it is not your job
> to take out the garbage, it is your job
> to empty the dishwasher. You are showing off again,
> exactly as you did in childhood—where
> is your sporting side, your famous
> ironic detachment? A little moonlight hits
> the broken window, a little summer moonlight, tender
> murmurs from the earth with its ready sweetnesses—
> is this the way you communicate
> with your husband, not answering
> when he calls, or is this the way the heart
> behaves when it grieves: it wants to be
> alone with the garbage? If I were you,
> I'd think ahead. After fifteen years,
> his voice could be getting tired; some night
> if you don't answer, someone else will answer.

Glück has done a household job nobody asked or wanted her to do, because she wanted to feel superior and alone: to identify with the moon and the moonlight, rather than with the broken windows. But the context—the garbage, the anger—makes the lines about moonlight angry too, makes them savage the tranquility Glück wants to achieve: "tender / murmurs from the earth with its ready sweetnesses" sounds over the top on purpose—it widens the arc of the next line's swing from lyricism into snappishness, thence back down into practical caution.

Here the series of potential endings is a series of progressively harsher rhetorical questions, each of which could have served as a climax. Glück could have closed the poem soon after "detachment," or "husband," or "calls," or "grieves": each choice to continue extends her chosen isolation. It is no wonder we leave the poem with Glück still on her own in the garage. Glück should (she feels) return to her husband because he will have affairs if she avoids him too assiduously, but she has been avoiding him in part because she already suspects him of wanting to sleep around. The half-rhymes and identical rhymes (*garage/garbage, job/job, moonlight/ moonlight*) stick and grate, and are meant to grate: the first two-thirds of the poem make a sound like a powerful motor trying to dislodge stuck wheels. It is also the sound of depressive realism, condemned (as it knows) to describe the wounds it cannot salve.

Glück remains in the garage because none of her thoughts has actually moved her to act any differently, to fend off that "someone else." The complaints naive readers make against poems like "Midnight"—that they offer no prescriptive ethics, no visionary consolation, and no plan for action—are complaints against depressive realism in general, against the accurate, stark depiction of persons for whom nothing can be done. Matthew Arnold excluded from his corpus one of his own long poems because, he wrote, in it "suffering finds no vent in action. . . . [In that poem] there is everything to be endured, nothing to be done."[11] Glück files almost exactly the same complaint against her own work in "Marina," from *Meadowlands:* "You took me to a place / where I could see the evil in my character / and left me there."[12]

Of the good work in *Meadowlands,* the poems called "Parables" will be easiest to anthologize, since they depend the least on the biographical, and mythical, contexts the book creates. "Parable of Flight" begins:

> A flock of birds leaving the side of the mountain.
> Black against the spring evening, bronze in early summer,
> rising over blank lake water.
>
> Why is the young man disturbed suddenly,
> his attention slipping from his companion?
> His heart is no longer wholly divided; he's trying to think
> how to say this compassionately.

The young man and his friend must be ending a romance. "Flock" chimes with "black" and "blank lake," "spring" with "evening," "summer" with "water"; when the first three lines with their flock of assonant nouns depart, we meet instead people whose lives sound far less harmonious than were the fugitive birds':

> Now we hear the voices of the others, moving through the
>   library
> toward the veranda, the summer porch; we see them

taking their usual places on the various hammocks and
    chairs,
the white wood chairs of the old house, rearranging
the striped cushions.

Does it matter where the birds go? Does it even matter
what species they are?
They leave here, that's the point,
first their bodies, then their sad cries.
And from that moment, cease to exist for us.

You must learn to think of our passion that way.
Each kiss was real, then
each kiss left the face of the earth.

In "Parable of Flight" the succession of potential endings is not temporal but spatial. The five stanzas make up four scenes, like the pan-
els of a screen or an altarpiece: birds, young-man-and-companion,
people-in-the-house, you-and-I. And Glück allots each scene its own
kind of verse: balanced groups of nouns for the birds, long talky lines
for the talky "others," Glück's ordinary clipped lineation for you-and-
I. With its parallel transience in parallel stanzas, its birds rising over the
close of the poem, and its triplet *leaving-leave-left,* the "Parable" invokes, faintly and ambitiously, Shakespeare's sonnet 73, Keats's "To
Autumn," and Yeats's wild swans, whose "hearts have not grown old,"
though they leave and return to Coole every year.[13] The kisses left, as
the romance ends, as the birds migrate away; the porch will lack them
all before the autumn has ended. Glück's lines contract from "taking
their usual places on the various hammocks and chairs" (six stresses
in seventeen syllables) to "They leave here, that's the point" (six in six)
as the poet's attention contracts to her own, narrow case.

In *Meadowlands,* as in her other books, Glück's assembled endings can follow from one another temporally, spatially, syllogisti-
cally, and even dialectically, as two or more sides of an argument.
Each stanza of "Parable of Flight" offers a "point" the next stanza
rejects; in "Parable of the Trellis," each version of the trellis-plus-
vine scene cancels the one before it. The latter poem begins:

    A clematis grew at the foot of a great trellis.
    Despite being
    modeled on a tree, the trellis
    was a human invention; every year, in May,

the green wires of the struggling vine
climbed the straightforward
trellis, and after many years
white flowers burst from the brittle wood, like
a star shower from the heart of the garden.

Enough of that ruse. We both know
how the vine grows without
the trellis, how it sneaks
along the ground; we have both seen it
flower there, the white blossoms
like headlights growing out of a snake.

Had the vine clung to the trellis—had it, literally, grown up—it
would have stood both for the poet's choice of a heroic "high" language (*struggling* vine, *straightforward* trellis, *star, heart*) and for the
choice most parents want their Telemachus-aged teens to make.
But this season the vine "sneaks along the ground," a Miltonic
snake rebelling, hiding from God's planned, adult light. If the white
flowers were *more* like headlights, they would show the vine the
way ahead, as if there were a road along the ground it could follow,
as if there were a well-marked route to adulthood which young
people could follow unaided. But there is no such route; the flowers of youthful willfulness shed little light, and Glück corrects herself again:

This isn't what the vine wants.
Remember, to the vine, the trellis
was never an image of confinement:
this is not
diminishment or tragedy.

The vine has a dream of light:
what is life in the dirt
with its dark freedoms
compared to supported ascent?

And for a time,
every summer we could see the vine
relive this decision, thus
obscuring the wood, structure
beautiful in itself, like
a harbor or willow tree.

Where other poets change moods by changing images or adjectives, Glück alters her pace: the vine's lines stop at syntactical breaks, the trellis's stop one word afterward (on *thus, structure, like*). "[L]ike / a harbor or willow tree," the trellis resembles more than anything a mother: the poem has become a "parable" about how a child's ostentatious, obvious development (or his refusal to develop) obscures a mother's. Having watched the backyard, and the first sentence of the poem, as if it were a photograph captioned "clematis," we are invited to see it now as "trellis," a perspective their surprising separation has made possible: the defense of poetic ambition has become a defense of bareness, and the parable of family life has yielded a story of the independence of a mother, unwillingly and lately achieved.

Though Glück has declared her devotion to self-remakings, the best poems in *Meadowlands* do not so much break Glück's older styles, or reject her former sensibilities, as shed light on her wish to break them, or make that wish their subject. In them Glück tries and fails to dispel her obsessions; they are poems of resignation and frustration at inevitable inwardness, inviting in, and then expelling, the outside world's wacky details. These moves create more ways to concatenate potential endings: Will the poem conclude by taking in, or by rejecting, its unfamiliar matter? Glück caps *Meadowlands* with a suite of poems that try to describe happiness, some in her novel talky forms, some in her more resonant old: this is a new project for her, and one most astonishing—and most successful— when it comes off as another renunciation, as in "Otis":

> A beautiful morning; nothing
> died in the night.
> The Lights are putting up their bean tepees.
> Rebirth! Renewal! And across the yard,
> very quietly, someone is playing Otis Redding.

The first line is the smallest, least ambitious concept of beauty anyone could have—a depressive realist's idea of a miracle: "nothing died." Glück again wants to make herself settle for scenes and loves anyone could get, and the tone the poem achieves mixes public acceptance with secret exasperation. The Lights are doing all right for themselves, taking actions, celebrating Succoth; they are happier in this world than Glück, who has to make herself exclaim "Rebirth!" with an exclamation point.

"Parable of the Gift," another poem about happiness, returns to the gardening motifs of *The Wild Iris*. The "gift" is a fuchsia plant, dead because Glück left it out overnight:

> I have
> killed my gift, exposed
> flowers in a mass of leaves,
> mistaking it
> for part of nature with
> its many stems: what
> do I do with you now,
> former living thing
> that last night still
> resembled my friend, abundant
> leaves like her fluffy hair
> although the leaves had
> a reddish cast: I see her
> climbing the stone steps in spring dusk
> holding the quivering
> present in her hands, with
> Eric and Daphne following
> close behind, each
> bearing a towel of lettuce leaves:
> so much, so much to celebrate
> tonight, as though she were saying
> here is the world, that should be
> enough to make you happy.

Here the sequence of potential endings proceeds backward in time, from the moment after the plant died, to the moment when Glück's friend gave it to her, to the moment when the nameless friend (along with "Eric and Daphne") approached with the gift. (One of the poems in *Ararat* works by backward progression, too: the new widow of "A Fantasy" "wants to be back in the cemetery, / back in the sickroom, the hospital"—but "not so far as the marriage, the first kiss.") The two- and three-beat lines stretch out, calm down, and turn more regular as Eric and Daphne enter with their ordinary lettuce. It's *not* much to celebrate—from the perspective of the dark garage most lives aren't—and the Glück who speaks most of the poem (and who offers its last four lines behind the double screen of subjunctive quotation) cannot bring herself either to celebrate or to reject the life she has.

Most readers of poetry will have heard before the question at the heart of "Parable of the Gift," the question the unimaginative acquaintance always asks the imaginative child: *Why aren't you happy with the world as it is?* If the poem describes Glück's particular disposition, it also evokes a more general dissatisfaction, what Samuel Johnson called "that hunger of imagination which preys incessantly upon life."[14] Expressed as a hunger at once for answers, for novelty, and for fixity, some such hunger has always been one of Glück's subjects, as surely as her biography has been another. Her poems of multiple endings, pressing on past the points where they might have stopped, embody the depressive realist's unasked-for skill at seeing past illusions, seeing through the conclusions with which others might have been happy.

Away from hope's delusive mine, those afflicted—or blessed—with depressive realism can seem to see through themselves and others, to know us better than we know ourselves. Their penalty is anhedonia: they see farthest because they have the least faith. Glück's poems fascinate me not least because she makes anhedonia interesting; her refusal of unusual words and elaborate phrases and the other demands she imposes on herself sound less like the elements of style than like its enemies, and yet what she calls her periodic "impoverishment" has given her not only her instantly recognizable attitude, but the self-correcting, self-stopping, unbreakably memorable structures which embody it.

NOTES

1. Experimental psychologists continue to test the hypothesis. A recent study concludes that *mildly* depressed people—but not those with clinical depression—are better at predicting certain events than those who are not depressed at all. See Ermine G. Kapci and Duncan Cramer, "The Accuracy of Dysphoric and Nondepressed Groups' Predictions of Life Events," *Journal of Psychology Interdisciplinary and Applied* 132 (November 1998): 659–71.

2. Helen Vendler, *The Music of What Happens* (Cambridge: Harvard University Press, 1988) 437.

3. George Eliot, *The Mill on the Floss*, ed. A. S. Byatt (London: Penguin, 1985) 485.

4. *The Triumph of Achilles* is included in *The First Four Books of Poems.*

5. Relevant to the matter of "Mock Orange," as to Glück in general, is Nancy Mairs's essay "On Not Liking Sex": "Afraid of being reduced by another to an object," Mairs writes, "I have persisted in seeing myself as

such." See *Plaintext* (Tucson: University of Arizona Press, 1986) 91. Subsequent references will appear in the text.

6. Barbara Herrnstein Smith, *Poetic Closure: A Study of How Poems End* (Chicago: University of Chicago Press, 1968) 157, 152, 177.

7. This is also a rhetorical strategy, since most of the essay objects to excessive indeterminacy in recent poetry, a quality which Glück associates with poets' use of incomplete sentences. See Louise Glück, "Ersatz Thought," *Threepenny Review* (winter 1999): 15.

8. Louise Glück, "Fear of Happiness," *PN Review* 118 (November–December 1997): 57.

9. Bonnie Costello also considers the poem a conflict between narrative and another mode: "The lyric's investment in the moment as an eternity, or rather, its elegiac sense of the present . . . gives us the figure at the beginning of 'Moonless Night.' . . . Glück will not ask us, as so many lyric poets do, to dwell on this fixed image forever. But nor is she especially concerned, as the strictly narrative artist must be, with conclusions." See "*Meadowlands:* Trustworthy Speakers," in this collection.

10. Calvin Bedient, "'Man Is Altogether Desire'?" *Salmagundi* 90–91 (1991): 217.

11. *Matthew Arnold: A Critical Edition of the Major Works,* ed. Miriam Allott and Robert H. Super (New York: Oxford University Press, 1986) 173.

12. The title and situation refer to the stranded, virtuous daughter in Shakespeare's *Pericles,* and perhaps to T. S. Eliot's poem of the same name. (For Glück on Eliot, see *Proofs & Theories,* 19–22.)

13. *The Collected Works of W. B. Yeats,* vol. 1, *The Poems,* ed. Richard Finneran (New York: Macmillan, 1989) 131.

14. *The Yale Edition of the Works of Samuel Johnson,* vol. 16, *Rasselas and Other Tales,* ed. Gwin J. Kolb (New Haven: Yale University Press, 1990) 118.

PAUL BRESLIN

Thanatos Turannos
The Poetry of Louise Glück

"'Tis sufficient to say, according to the proverb, that *here is God's plenty,*" wrote John Dryden in praise of Chaucer. So Louise Glück must be our anti-Chaucer (not "anti" as simply against, but as in "antimatter," something whose entire condition of being is opposite to that of the contrasting term). Here is God's dearth; endure it if you can. The poems rest on a seemingly metaphysical conviction that plenitude is contamination, desire a humiliating surrender of autonomy, and pleasure a fleeting distraction that leaves us no better off—if we're lucky—and usually worse. She has written eloquently in defense of poets such as T. S. Eliot who have been criticized as "enem[ies] of the life force" (*Proofs & Theories,* 19). She admires George Oppen because he "regularly defines things by saying what they are not. This method of creation by eradication is, for me, congenial" (*Proofs & Theories,* 82). She prefers Robinson Jeffers, whose "declared metaphor for . . . earth, the 'massive mysticism of stone,' is elimination," to Czeslaw Milosz, whose relatively benign vision is "maternal. Earth centered. Moon centered. Fruitful. Predictable. Cyclical" (*Proofs & Theories,* 66). Even Rilke, a poet her own work sometimes reminds me of, is not quite pure enough in his negation: "To read Eliot, for me, is to feel the presence of the abyss; to read Rilke is to sense the mattress under the window" (*Proofs & Theories,* 21). She shares with the embittered Old Man of Yeats's *Purgatory* a contempt of "Fat, greasy life."

It is a position most of us cannot inhabit, but we need to enter it from time to time and allow its corrosives to drip on our most cherished illusions, which will either dissolve (in which case, good riddance) or metamorphose into firmer things. Blake wrote, in *The Marriage of Heaven and Hell,* that "one portion of being is the Prolific, the other, the Devouring. . . . / But the Prolific would cease to be Prolific unless the Devourer as a sea received the excess of his delights. . . . // These two classes of men are always upon earth, &

they should be enemies; whoever tries to reconcile them seeks to destroy existence."[1] Louise Glück says, memorably, what can be said from the Devourer's perspective, which is the minority tradition in our age of openness, heteroglossia, and inclusion. Blake warns us against attempts at reconciliation, but encourages us to think of each "class" as a necessary dialectical corrective to the other. And those of us who harbor both of these adversaries unreconciled within us will want to engage with Louise Glück's poems.

I. The Emergence of Glück's Mature Style:
Firstborn, The House on Marshland, Descending Figure

Glück's debut volume, *Firstborn* (1968), is the one I can do without. As many critics have remarked,[2] she departed from its style in her second book, *The House on Marshland* (1975), and never looked back. Its excesses may have been necessary, however, to exorcise the blandishments of plenitude, especially those conventionally reserved for women: sexual fulfillment, marriage, childbearing, the domesticity of house and garden. Not that these do not remain among her prominent subjects, but never again does she seem so fragilely defended against them, so quick to erupt into a theatrical contempt that protests too much, and too loudly: "I saw her pulsing crotch . . . the lice rooted in that baby's hair" ("The Chicago Train"); "Saw you throbbing / In my syrups" ("Hesitate to Call"); "I watch him drive into the gored / Roasts" ("The Edge"); "Women oozing from their stays / Go wild" ("Portrait of the Queen in Tears"); "I watch your hands pulling at the grapes" ("The Islander"); "In Westchester, the crocus spreads like cancer" ("Easter Season"). Fat, greasy life blights everything, including the speaker's own body with its sexual "syrups." These poems are less a critique of plenitude, as a moral or aesthetic ideal, than a panicked outcry against its threatening encroachments.

In the seven years between *Firstborn* and *The House on Marshland,* there had "grown upon her," as Calvin Bedient writes, "insidiously and strengtheningly . . . an 'infamous calm.'"[3] Glück writes in a quiet, laconic voice so calm, given the implied intensity of what it evokes, as to seem numb, traumatized. Although she has written of her fascination with "the possibilities of context" and her "preoccupation with syntax" (*Proofs & Theories,* 4, 8), the poems of the second volume tend strongly toward parataxis. In this respect they sound a little like the poetry of Merwin or Strand from about the same period, but instead of offering a parable or a dreamlike set of images, they usually imply a narrative that has been withheld, an incompletely recovered context (the seven lines of "Under Taurus," for instance, imply a narrative of a lover's desire once resisted, now accepted).[4] Their attitude toward syntax contrasts strongly with another poet Glück might be compared to, Emily Dickinson. No less than Glück, Dickinson seems to have "loved those poems that seemed so small on the page but that swelled in the mind," and both have created poems that "haunt because they are not whole, though wholeness is implied" (*Proofs & Theories*, 4, 73). But within the spare symmetries of Dickinson's quatrains, her syntax bristles with hypotactic energy: subjunctives, embedded subordinate clauses, sentences spilling over lines and stanza breaks. Her syntax beats against the metrical form as the soul beats against the "magic prison" (J. 1601) of fleshly embodiment. In contrast, some of Glück's poems move in unbroken strings of declarative sentences (e.g., "The Fortress," from *The House on Marshland*). When she does connect the parts, she favors "and" or temporal conjunctions such as "then" rather than subordinate clauses, although when she does use subordination, it often has heightened force because it has been used sparingly.

Two of the most-discussed poems in the second book, "All Hallows" and "Still Life," make good illustrations of Glück's typical way of moving through a poem at this period. "Still Life" is just eight lines long:

> Father has his arm around Tereze.
> She squints. My thumb
> is in my mouth: my fifth autumn.
> Near the copper beech
> the spaniel dozes in shadows.
> Not one of us does not avert his eyes.
>
> Across the lawn, in full sun, my mother
> stands behind her camera.

If this were not a still life but a Lowellian life study, we would know, from other poems if not from this one, who "Tereze" is; here, the one proper name in the poem stands unexplained next to the generic father, mother, and family dog, who, though the breed is specified, is unnamed and could be either male or female. The "his" of the sixth line is gender neutral, taking in the whole family group. From the observed fact that a photographer does not shoot into the light, Glück creates a rift between the camera-wielding mother and the family she wants to capture on film. The eyes are averted, one infers, from more than the sun, and the white space between the first six lines and the last two represents more than the width of the lawn, the difference between sunlight and shadow, or the leap from the images still visible within the picture to the photographer, whose image does not appear within it but had to be there for the picture to exist at all. The mother's gaze, doubled by her camera, is too controlling, too unreciprocal, and it is from this aggression as much as the sunlight that all in the picture avert their eyes and hide in the shadows. Exactly why they feel the camera's scrutiny, and hers, to be obtrusive we do not learn; it is enough that we recognize a familiar kind of mute family tension at work in the scene.

"All Hallows" is twice as long and more complex. It opens by evoking a process already under way: "Even now this landscape is assembling." As the late-October setting implied by the title would warrant, it is a scene of depletion. The day ends as "the hills darken," and the oxen, lately busy in the fields, "sleep in their blue yoke." The harvest has been gathered, leaving the fields "picked clean," and an ominously "toothed moon" ascends. But the image of "the sheaves / bound evenly and piled at the roadside" suggests a plenitude carefully winnowed from this barrenness. Hovering somewhere far in the background is Keats's "To Autumn," except that the fullness of autumn's compensatory "music" has been stripped away as mercilessly as "the songs of Spring." What Glück's poem does share with Keats's Ode is the linking of death, exhaustion, and depletion with ripeness, harvest, and plenitude. It reveals, to quote a more recent ancestor, "the barrenness / Of the fertile thing that can attain no more."[5] Or is it, in Glück's sparer version, the fertility of the barren thing that can renounce no more?

The syntax of the first seven lines of "All Hallows," though not intricate, does nest some qualifiers within its statements. We're told that the oxen sleep, "the fields having been picked clean." Only then may the oxen rest from their labors. And although the floating participial construction leaves room for uncertainty, it would appear that the sheaves have been stacked at the end of the day, "as the toothed moon rises." The next two lines baldly assert a definition, yet leave open two opposite meanings, as if to undermine the aggressive certainty of the declarative syntax: "This is the barrenness /

of harvest or pestilence." The remainder of the poem is an un-
parseable sentence, suspending a heavily modified noun phrase with
no predicate:

> And the wife leaning out of the window
> with her hand extended, as in payment,
> and the seeds
> distinct, gold, calling
> *Come here*
> *come here, little one*
>
> And the soul creeps out of the tree.

We see "the wife" in a frozen gesture, leaning out from the domestic space of the house toward the assembling landscape. Then the
poem ends in a blur of grammatical relations. Are the seeds in the
extended hand or somewhere else? Are they the payment, or something distinct from it? Is it they or the wife who is "calling"? The
last line joins what would be a complete sentence ("the soul creeps
out of the tree") to the suspended noun phrase that has still not
reached its verb. The only subject to receive a predicate here is
"soul": the response is more active than the participial call, and the
soul rather than the supplicant has agency. The paratactic looseness
of the phrasing contributes to the sense of closure, which is felt as
an abandonment of analysis and control, so that what happens appears inevitable and inexplicable.

Though the haunting sense of incompleteness, things left unsaid
or unexplained, contributes to the suggestiveness of the poem, the
aesthetic of exclusion needs to be distinguished from mere vague-
ness, and if Glück had never written a better poem than "All Hallows," I would not admire her work as much as I do. One doesn't
want to be given everything coarsely and explicitly, but one does
want to be able, after patiently revisiting a poem, to be admitted
gradually into a few of its secrets. With this one, I don't find much
on the tenth reading that wasn't there in the first; it's a striking
mood piece that withholds so much of its motive for utterance that
its language seems in excess of its occasion.

It's with *Descending Figure* (1980) that Glück becomes a poet I
must read, rather than one of many talented, intermittently interesting writers who hover at the edge of my awareness. Its best-known
poem, though not necessarily its best, opens the book and has a

power to disturb that nothing in the first two collections matches. It inspired Greg Kuzma to denounce it as morally insensitive and technically incompetent,[6] and while I disagree with him, he is not mistaken to find something shocking in this meditation on death and childhood. It is possible to admire the poem and still not want to think its thought for very long, or very often. "The Drowned Children" opens with the words "You see," which Kuzma takes as bullying the reader to agree with what follows, but which might also be taken as a plea to listen to an argument few of us want to hear:

> You see, they have no judgment.
> So it is natural that they should drown,
> first the ice taking them in
> and then, all winter, their wool scarves
> floating behind them as they sink
> until at last they are quiet.
> And the pond lifts them in its manifold dark arms.

The title of the book's first section, "The Garden," does not prepare us for this: not nurturing and growth, but untimely death. The wool scarves would tug at the heartstrings in a conventional, even maudlin way, evoking a mother's fruitless attempt to protect her children, were it not that the killing elements parody the gestures of maternal care: the ice takes the children in; the pond holds them in its "manifold" arms, whereas a human mother can offer only two. "[A]t last they are quiet," as if, despite some complaints about bedtime, they have finally fallen asleep, leaving their parents free to relax.

If this drowning were evoked in the language of the nineteenth century, we would have a familiar Romantic consolation: the children would have "awakened from the dream of life" (Shelley), to be "Laved in the flood of thy bliss O death" (Whitman), while the living would "hear [them] where the waters run" (Tennyson).[7] But it is too late in the historical day for all that; besides, there is nothing like the ecstatic surge of the nineteenth-century poets' language in Glück's lines. As in "All Hallows," the verbs hang suspended as participles, until the pond finally gets the active predicate, "lifts." The life-taking water has more agency than the parents who cared for the children, who have the least agency of all. The children drown because it is "natural" for them, as beings not yet imbued with "judgment," to do.[8] The language of shelter and care assigned to the elements can only be a sentimental projection that the poem ruthlessly exposes as such.

The poem refuses the Romantic consolation of reabsorption into nature and asks the harsh question that goes back to Sophocles: is it best never to be born? Having been born only recently, the children have less to lose, and so "death must come to them differently." It is "the rest," their brief lives, that "is dreamed"—again recalling Shelley, but without the triumphal union with the white light behind the dome of many-colored glass. No one's soul is going to beacon like a star. Instead, the dead enter a suspended state, "blind and weightless," with at most a faint memory of "the lamp, / the good white cloth that covered the table, / their bodies." The dream is filled not with splendors but with minimal comforts: the lamp's artificial, indoor light; the cloth as bare adornment for the table where food was served and family gathered, or as covering for the vulnerable body. If these images are, to the living reader, poignant reminders of what death has taken, the poem gives no sign that the dead themselves remember these things, or regret their loss. Death—like birth in Wordsworth's Intimations Ode—"is but a sleep and a forgetting." And yet, as for Wordsworth, it is not complete forgetfulness, since the drowned children still "hear the names they used." The name, the first thing given at birth, is the last to disappear in death.

When Glück compares the names to "lures," they become talismanic: a name not only acknowledges a child, but serves as a magical spell leading the child back from death. Of course the parents want their child back; and of course the instinctive point of view, for the reader, is to side with the longing parents. But the poem refuses, and the perversity of that refusal accounts for a moral response like Kuzma's. If the names are lures, then the living are like fishermen, trying to capture the dead by guile.[9] The last three lines, in italics, are a translation, into the language of the living, of what the drowned children hear:

> *What are you waiting for*
> *come home, come home, lost*
> *in the waters, blue and permanent.*

But it is seductively beautiful to be lost in the waters, to be absorbed into something free of the constrictions of definite form, the color of purity. And death is permanence, whereas to be alive is to be fragile and transitory. These lines are themselves water-like in their syntactical indeterminacy. They begin by begging the children to come home, but the phrase "lost / in the waters, blue and permanent" has no firm grammatical connection to what precedes it. Are the children called home *from* the waters in which they are lost, or does coming home mean dissolving their identity altogether and *becoming* lost in the waters forever? Is "home" to be found in life or in death?

The calm, almost stunned tone of this poem does not suggest, to me, an aloof detachment, but mute astonishment at the fragility of life. All that separates a child who still sits by the lamp from one who has drowned is a thin sheet of ice that held, or gave way. The tone is not too far removed from that of the voice in *The Waste Land* that says: "I could not / Speak, and my eyes failed, I was neither / Living nor dead, and I knew nothing, / Looking into the heart of light, the silence." The deadened affect is a sign of terror, not indifference.

In *Descending Figure,* Glück's fascination "with the possibilities of context" shows itself in the way her poems talk to each other, so that repeated words or motifs gain a cumulative resonance, while "order and sequence . . . articulate a wider, more encompassing treatment of themes than that found in any single poem."[10] So when "Origins," in the sequence "The Garden," begins "As though a voice were saying / *you should be asleep by now*—" we remember the drowned children, "at last . . . quiet," and both lines resonate in "For My Sister," from the title sequence: "The dead ones are like that, / always the last to quiet." Faint reverberations are still heard when "The Dream of Mourning" begins "I sleep so you will be alive," and all of these usages trouble the assertion, in "Autumnal," that "the scattered dead / unite in one consuming vision of order." Out of context, this last assertion sounds like Eliot making a redemptive sacrament of history, both early ("Tradition and the Individual Talent") and late ("Little Gidding": "These men, and those who opposed them / And those whom they opposed / Accept the constitution of silence / and are folded in a single party"). In context, however, it sounds more ominous: the vision of order is "consuming" in other senses besides all-encompassing: it devours (and, given the importance of hunger and eating in Glück's poetry, that meaning stands out unignorably); it makes a false peace by getting the troublesome dead to shut up at last, the way parents coax cranky children to sleep.

Then there is the motif of the hand, which, the husband

promises in "Epithalamium," "*will not harm you,*" though so much else suggests that it will: in childhood, the speaker of "Tango" recalls, she and her sister would "sit under the table" while "the adults' hands / drum on our heads." She would laugh "a stark laugh" that meant "she's realized / that he [her father] never touches her. / She is a child; he could touch her / if he wanted to."[11] The patriarchal authority of fathers and grandfathers over daughters and grand-daughters merges with that of husbands over wives in "Grand-mother," when the granddaughter tries to see her grandfather from her grandmother's perspective, as the young husband he once was. Despite his apparently sincere tenderness, his kiss "might as well have been / his hand over her mouth." In "Aubade," a woman feels the "hunger" of a gull's cry as the man's "hand inside" her, an image of sexual penetration perhaps, but also of violated autonomy. In "World Breaking Apart," a man is "reaching for his wife's hand / across a slatted table, and quietly covering it"; later in the poem, it is her hand that rests on his chest, but the other, "the free hand," is "pain," while in the next poem, "The Return," after the breakup of the relationship, "a boy touched me on the street," yet "his hands were yours, / so gently making their murderous claim." No won-der the post-Edenic couple in "Covenant" are terrified as their child "reached its hands" toward them for comfort, and "they un-derstood they were mother and father, / there was no authority over them." Despite the tenderest intentions, parents hurt children, husbands hurt wives; the hand that reaches out for comfort will receive—or dispense—cruelty as well. The alternatives are the au-tonomy of the anorexic, that will take nothing from outside the self, or the inevitable violation that is the price of relational exis-tence. The significance of the call, "*come home, come home,*" in "The Drowned Children" expands over the course of the book, through echoes like these lines in "Tango":

> In the other room
> our parents merged into the one
> totemic creature:
> *Come,* she said. *Come to Mother.*
> You stood. You tottered toward
> the inescapable body.

The totemic parent-creature absorbs the father into the mother. "[T]he inescapable body" is not only the mother's body: it is the very fact of embodiment, of being "an object," as Charles Olson said a man (or woman) is, and therefore being in unavoidable relation to a physical world. "The Drowned Children" have escaped that condition and will not come back.

II. Ontology and Politics: An Excursus on Anorexia, Style, and Meaning

The social texture of Glück's poetry is thinner than that of any other poet who impresses me so much. One could reconstruct, by reading it, virtually none of the events, cultural shifts, or even changes of literary fashion in the nearly twenty years that separate *Descending Figure* from *Vita Nova* (1999). Nonetheless, it touches repeatedly, if indirectly, on gender politics, an intensely charged subject during that span, and never more so than in its autobiographical allusions to Glück's early struggles with anorexia nervosa. More critics have seized on this theme than on any other aspect of the poetry. Leslie Heywood takes her title for a book on "the anorexic aesthetic in modern culture" from Glück's poem "Dedication to Hunger," quoting, as epigraph, its much-revisited lines:

> touching, at fifteen,
> the interfering flesh
> that I would sacrifice
> until the limbs were free
> of blossom and subterfuge: I felt
> what I feel now, aligning these words—
> it is the same need to perfect, . . .

The poem itself makes the connection between the artist's striving for aesthetic perfection and the anorexic's desire to escape the interference of flesh. But to what extent do Glück's poems imply a critique of "modern culture," and to what extent do they conceive of embodiment as a metaphysical sullying, apart from the cultural demands of bodily self-denial placed on young women?

The avoidance of contingent particularity that gives the poems resonance can also leave them more indeterminate, more Rorschachesque than most. Even as they rigorously exclude the nonessential detail, they jettison the usual defenses against the intellectual will of the critic. Sometimes, they almost dissolve in their polyvalency, as if they too longed to escape from having a body, with its clear, finite boundaries making it visible and therefore vulnerable. At their best, they commit themselves far enough to achieve "the power of ruins," of "works of art either damaged or incomplete" (*Proofs & Theories,* 74). At other times, they refuse fully to exist as poems, not so much incomplete as inchoate. They can mean too many things to mean any of them forcefully.[12] Even the motivic repetition that extends beyond individual books can do only so much. If, for instance, we come back to "All Hallows" in *The House on Marshland* fresh from study of the motif of the maternal call to the child in *Descending Figure,* it remains hard to say whether, as Elizabeth Dodd would have it, the poem is at the literal level about "the creation of children" or about something else: the invocation of the poetic muse, or the conjuring of the lost sister from the dead. If one tries to ground the poems in the social, in what Ludwig Binswanger would call the *Mitwelt,*[13] they can slide like eels from one's grasp. Contributing to this elusiveness is the half-unmooring of metaphors from their physical basis, noted by Kuzma when he complains that lures don't in fact slip across the pond. To register the force of "lures" in "The Drowned Children," one must think of fishing, but thinking too literally about fishing will spoil the effect.

In looking at the treatment of anorexia and female embodiment in the poems, one might take a range of positions. Although Elizabeth Dodd cites Susie Orbach's argument that anorexia is a symbolic protest against the contradictory demands placed on women (to be always concerned with nurturing others while denying appetites of their own), Orbach also makes a broader argument that anorexia is a metaphor of "our" time. The collectivity signified by "our" appears to extend beyond women, although it is in the anorexic woman's struggle that the contradictions of the times become most sharply visible: "The starvation amidst plenty, the denial set against desire, the striving for invisibility versus the wish to be seen—these key features of anorexia—are a metaphor for our age."[14] Heywood pushes the cultural figuration even further, finding in literary modernism a shift "from female disease to textual ideal" (60), to be found in male writers such as Kafka and Eliot who worked long before the post–World War II developments in child-rearing that, for Orbach, account for the increased incidence of anorexia from the early 1960s onward. Drawing on the work of Susan Bordo,[15] Heywood places Glück among the "philosophical anorexics," "women who have internalized the dictates of the philosophical tradition and accepted them as truths" (40), so that their anorexia becomes an extension of the devaluation of the flesh to be found in Western philosophers such as Plato and Augustine. Heyward credits Glück with making the process of internalization "explicit, thereby producing an 'alienation effect' to that process" (41), but remains troubled that "rather than using anorexia as a strategy of protest, she leaves the definition of female body as lack firmly in place" (46). Similarly, Lynn Keller concludes her discussion of the poems up through *The Triumph of Achilles* by observing that "Glück has not passed beyond self-loathing, and this makes reading her work still a profoundly uncomfortable experience. Yet it would be false to conclude that in Glück's case the ongoing nature of her struggle has greatly restricted the power of her art; on the contrary, one could argue that this inner battle is precisely what electrifies her poetry. . . . Feminist scholarship will be enriched by remaining in touch with the varied perspectives of the many women writing today, including those like Louise Glück, whose poetry raises crucial, disturbing questions about women's complicity in their own oppression."[16]

In our time, most people want poetry to resist oppression, to make things happen as Auden said it couldn't. Or at least we want it to recognize and name oppression as such. So, I suppose, do I, and yet perhaps we are asking too much. Or not enough: it is easier, even where it is justified, to denounce states of self-torment as politically inflicted than to render unforgettably what it feels like to experience them. A few poets, at their rare best, have been able to judge and evoke in the same poem. It's a synthesis I used to demand, but the standard now strikes me as impossibly severe, best understood as an ideal to aspire toward with the full realization that one is unlikely to reach it. When Glück writes about her "dedication to hunger," her powers of evocation exceed her powers of self-knowledge, but that limitation seems preferable to its opposite, the ability to analyze and judge without conjuring into language the *affect* of the experience being examined. So, to return to the passage that gave both Lynn Keller and Susan Heyward the titles of their critiques, what impresses me is the stubborn affirmation that as the speaker once felt at fifteen she feels now in the act of writing the poem. She still experiences the "sacrifice" of the body's sexual flowering as a way of becoming "free," the enjambed line break suggesting a freedom-to as well as the freedom-from that the rest of the sentence describes. The poem doesn't repent, nor does it ignore the extreme cost of its renunciation, "aligning" the words "blossom" and "subterfuge" as two faces of the same enemy. If you want a sense of what it would be like to experience your body in this way, Glück can tell you; if you want to understand why a woman of our time might experience her body in this way, read the shrinks and sociologists.

In my admittedly hurried attempt to swot up anorexia nervosa for this section of my chapter, the study that resonated most powerfully with Glück's poetry was Binswanger's famous case history of Ellen West, already mined by Frank Bidart for one of his finest poems. Ellen West aspired to be a poet, and Binswanger extensively analyzes her writings as a key to the phenomenology of her illness. Binswanger insists on refraining from moral judgment of Ellen West's attitudes or behavior, including her suicide. He treats the disease as something that, after a few early momentous choices, became a closed world, fated beyond cure. When Ellen West's husband agreed to her confinement in a padded cell only if the doctor thought he could eventually cure or at least notably ameliorate her illness, Binswanger released her, knowing that she would probably take her own life soon after, as indeed she did, and he defends this outcome as the only possible resolution of her existence as it had then evolved: "In her death we perceive with especial impressiveness the existential meaning, or more accurately contra-meaning, of her life" (297). His study oddly mixes numbing pedantry and abstraction with almost preternatural empathy and attention to the nuances of his patient's language. Its politics, to the extent it betrays any, are disturbing to a twenty-first-century reader: what Orbach or Heywood would analyze as socially constructed gender roles, Binswanger assigns to the fated realm of Heideggerian "thrownness" [*Geworfenheit*]: Ellen West's existence is at odds with "its actual thrownness into the role of woman" (271), a formulation that allows no distinction between "role" and female embodiment. He questions his patient's "equations" of "slender = higher spiritual (soft, blond, Aryan) type, fat = bourgeois Jewish type," but not the racial typologies themselves (316).

If you are interested in the interaction between social forms and personal suffering, Binswanger is at best unhelpful, at worst collusive in obscuring the connection. But I finish his study with an overwhelming sense of having been shown an interiority that would have been unimaginable to me without his mediation. And that is akin to what I derive from Glück's poems, except that here the mediation has been achieved by the same person who has endured the experience, and that in itself is a significant achievement. Readers in our time tend to look for confirmation of themselves in what they read, and in doing so they suppose they are affirming diversity, their right to their own way of existence. But surely we learn more about the astonishing variety of experience by looking for what is unlike ourselves: the best book may not be the one in which I see myself revealed, but the one in which I enter another subjectivity I could not have begun to imagine without another's help.

III. The Uses and Limits of Mythology: Telemachus and His Parents

Of Glück's five books since *Descending Figure,* two—*Meadowlands* (1996) and *Vita Nova* (1999)—make extensive use of mythical allusion. Poems about Circe, Penelope, Odysseus, and Telamachus, about Orpheus and Eurydice, Dido and Aeneas, or Paolo and Francesca, provide impersonal analogues for autobiographical narrative. Sometimes the myth-based poems are juxtaposed with others, more directly autobiographical, set in the present. Sometimes the distinction between mythical antiquity and our own world collapses, so that Penelope can allude to Maria Callas ("Penelope's Song," in *Meadowlands*). Glück's first extensive foray into mythology occurs in *The Triumph of Achilles* (1985), though that collection is not so pervasively structured by mythical analogues as the later two.

Elizabeth Dodd places Glück in a tradition of "personal classicism," which "combine[s] personal impulses (those that appear in confessional poetry) with careful elements of control that allow them to shape and frame—and mute—what are at their core romantic, personal poems. Those elements chosen to mitigate the personal center tend specifically to mute or conceal the autobiographical details in the poetry and to imply a more 'universal' approach." This mode, she claims, has been especially favored by women who "have found themselves in the quandary Adrienne Rich describes: 'I had been taught that poetry should be "universal," which meant, of course, nonfemale. . . . I had tried very much *not* to identify myself as a female poet'" (1–2). But one can believe that mythical allusion provides common ground without believing that it does so because the experiences recounted in myths are universally shared; rather, if one is familiar with the treatment of the same myth by other writers, one sees the new adaptation in relation to that tradition. It is a return to oft-visited material, but if the new treatment is not dully derivative, some new emphasis, interpretation, or narrative perspective will revise or challenge our sense of what the myth means. So Glück gives us Telemachus brooding on the dynamics of his parents' marriage, or Eurydice's descent to the underworld seen from her point of view rather than that of Orpheus. These poems, by borrowing a plot from the classical source, can make a narrative parable of what in other poems can only appear as a lyrical and phenomenological rendering of states of feeling. They are more accessible but at the same time less distinctive on the whole than my favorite Glück poems. They are more like what other poets have done, and sometimes done better. Nonetheless, they introduce an element of playfulness, even wit, that provides a welcome contrast to the usual dark solemnity. They can provide an interpretive frame for some of the more oracular lyrics, as long as one doesn't trust them too far. They represent Glück in her most public, extroverted mode—which is of course not to say that they are public or extroverted in manner, only that they are less uncompromising in their refusal of those qualities than the rest of her work. My reservation concerning most of them is that where one hopes to find the myth reinterpreting a private experience, or the private experience reinterpreting the myth, one finds instead the private experience flattened or moralized by the received meanings of the myth, which can be clarifying but is not especially interesting. The mythological poems that most escape this limitation, I find, are those in the "Odyssey" sequence in *Meadowlands,* especially those spoken by Telemachus.

Glück's fascination with Telemachus intrigues me. Like Mozart's coldly honorable Don Ottavio, Telemachus tends to put people off. After fighting by his father's side against the suitors, he disappears into the woodwork of the palace, his adventures finished no sooner than begun. Tennyson's Ulysses damns him with faint praise as "blameless . . . centered in the sphere / Of common duties, decent not to fail / In offices of tenderness, and pay / Meet adoration to my household gods." He is not the stuff of which further epics can be made. Only in Joyce's incarnation, as Stephen Dedalus, does Telemachus begin to emerge from his father's shadow. Glück's Telemachus is obsessed with his parents' marriage. In contrast to Joyce's defiant adolescent, he seems to be child and youth at once, combining a young man's intellectual development with a child's imprisonment in the domestic sphere. Telemachus has become that familiar contemporary figure, the analysand, trying to keep his illusions down to a dull roar, to unknot his identity from the entanglements of his upbringing.

His first appearance in "Telemachus' Detachment" is not promising; one fears that myth will serve mainly as a defense mechanism. "[L]ooking / at [his] parents' lives," he once "thought heartbreaking," but now would add "also / insane. Also / very funny." This conclusion is too arch for wisdom, too bald for wit. But when he returns as speaker in "Telemachus' Guilt," he provides the critique of his own detachment: he recognizes that he was "proud of [his] father / for staying away," and would "smile / when [his] mother wept." He concludes by hoping "she understood how like / her own coldness it was, / a means of remaining / separate from what / one loves deeply." Here, he recognizes detachment as a kind of aggression, though undertaken initially in self-defense, that he has learned from his parents: from his father's "staying away" and from his mother's inhuman calm in the face of abandonment. He sees that "Patience of the sort [his] mother / practised on [his] father" is not a "tribute," as Odysseus "in his self- / absorption thought," but rather "a species of rage." This insight sheds light on earlier poems, especially those of *Ararat* (1990), in which the marriage of the speaker's parents, and her relation to her parents, are described in similar terms, where mother, father, and daughter all find ways to use detachment as a shield against the pain of rejected love or encroaching mortality. "Long ago, I was wounded," *Ararat* begins and ends, but by the end of the book, the daughter realizes that her pain did not mean she "was not loved," but rather that she herself "loved."

Telemachus, entering manhood, has a hard act to follow. Neither in Homer nor in Glück does he have any girlfriends, and in "Telemachus' Fantasy" he is acutely aware of his father's fabled dalliances with Circe, Calypso, and Nausicaa; he struggles to understand why Odysseus was "so attractive / to women," even "women / so much younger than he was." His hypothesis, that "women like to see a man / still whole, still standing, but / about to go to pieces: such / disintegration reminds them / of passion," puts women in the position of sexual aggressors, never so aroused as by the man's imminent destruction, which presumably their attentions will accelerate. They are like Maenads about to light into Orpheus. Such an interpretation reveals not only a fear, tinged also with contempt, of female desire, but a wish to envision the male as the pursued rather than the pursuer, reversing the conventional gender roles so as to absolve himself of the need to initiate sexual relationships. But although his fantasy is to become, like his father, so desirable that women will simply offer themselves to him, he realizes that he is not destined for life on the edge. He will never have the glamorous aura of the man "about to go to pieces," and he knows it. "I never / wish for my father's life," he says, but his own imaginings belie him. Of course he does, and perhaps for that reason he needs to construct an elegant moral argument proving that his father's life is not enviable. Again he makes the gesture that, by now, we recognize as Glück's characteristic move: in a defiant assertion of his autonomy, he disavows emotions that, against his will, his own utterance helplessly reveals.

Telemachus needs to believe that he understands his father better than his father himself ever can. Just as Odysseus mistakes Penelope's angry patience for "tribute," so too he is "dazzled" (with its literal sense of "blinded") by the sexual attention showered upon him. "Is it / fortunate," Telemachus asks, "to encounter circumstances / so responsive to one's own will . . . ?" No, of course not; better to avoid the curse of going "unthwarted," lest one "believe oneself / entirely good or worthy." Better undeluded than happy. Besides, the illusion must disintegrate soon enough, as "either / one becomes a monster or / the beloved sees what one is." Odysseus, with his celebrated appetite for "Life piled on life" (so Tennyson), is on the side of Eros and the Prolific. Telemachus must cut him down to size in order to keep his own asceticism from looking mean-spirited by comparison. But the end of the poem outruns his control. It would be "Less dangerous / to believe" his father was "drawn to" the women who detained him "and so stayed / to see who they were," but imagination, with its dangers, has the last word: "I think, though, / as an imaginative man / to some extent he / became who they were." To entertain this thought, Telemachus must himself "think . . . / as an imaginative man" for a moment. (The syntax is ambiguous enough so that "as an imaginative man" may seem at first to refer backward to "I" rather than forward to "he.") As his father became what the seducing women were, Telemachus becomes for a moment what his seductive father is. In so doing, he confronts the dissolution of autonomy and identity that haunts Glück's poetry early and late: he is not the sort of man to permit such a dissolution, but he can glimpse what it would be like.

In his last two monologues, "Telemachus' Confession" and "Telemachus' Burden," the son draws the boundary around his identity without claiming the spurious "detachment" he professes in the first. In "Telemachus' Confession," it is not immediately clear what he must confess. But the guilty secret seems to be his recognition that although his parents "were not better off" after his father's departure for Troy, he himself was. What was for them suffering and deprivation was, for him, an opportunity. His maturation had been delayed because "long into adulthood [he] retained / something of the child's / hunger for ritual." "Hunger" is the recurring sign in Glück of dependency, debilitating need, invaded autonomy. It can take the form of sexual hunger, which requires another person to satiate it, or in this case, the child's "sense of being / insufficiently loved," which requires a constant return to the parents in the hope of at last receiving what has been withheld. For Telemachus, this hunger is further complicated because it is doubled:

> they each wanted something
> different from me: having
> to fabricate the being
> each required in any
> given moment was
> less draining than
> having to be
> two people.

He is "better off" after his father's departure because he now answers to only one set of demands. Whether because of that simplification or merely because enough time has passed, he eventually "realized I *was* / actually a person," rather than a reactive fabrication designed to win sufficient love at last. Having acquired his own "voice" and "perceptions," though he "came to them late," Telemachus need "no longer regret / the terrible moment in the fields, / the ploy that took / my father away." This statement circles back to the recognition at the opening of the poem: if his father's departure helped him to acquire selfhood, of course he cannot regret it, though as a dutiful son he would be expected to do so. It is that absence of dutiful regret that he confesses.

In the last of his monologues, "Telemachus' Burden," the son accepts the intractability of his circumstances. He is able to criticize his parents more frankly than in the earlier poems, having dealt with his "guilt" and made his "confession," but the burden remains.

He says that his mother, had she "been capable of honesty / . . . would have been / a Stoic." But as a queen, she needs to believe she has had the power to command, and so has "chosen / her own destiny." But "She would have had to be / insane to choose that destiny." At last we understand why he thinks that his parents' life was insane as well as heartbreaking. Either Penelope indeed has chosen her destiny, which would be insane, or she has deluded herself into believing that she chose it, which would only be another form of insanity. As for Odysseus, he fares no better in his son's assessment:

> Well,
>
> good luck to my father, in my opinion
> a stupid man if he expects
> his return to diminish
> her isolation; perhaps
> he came back for that.

So much for the fabled craftiness of Odysseus. If he expects his return to bring Penelope out of her isolation, he is stupid, but if he comes back in order to subject himself to her isolation, he is scarcely less so. As Telemachus finishes speaking, he has accomplished the rebellion needed to separate himself from his parents, though with all sorts of burdened requests for and dispensations of forgiveness.

The "Odyssey" sequence, with monologues by Circe and Penelope as well as Telemachus—Odysseus, though spoken of, does not speak—is interspersed with other kinds of poetry, including a series of "parables" and, as if in parallel to the Odyssey monologues, conversation poems spoken by unmythologized contemporary figures, most notably by a husband and wife who appear to be analogous with Odysseus and Penelope. These dialogue poems are full of an edgy, reproachful wit that suggests great intimacy but also long-harbored bitterness between the two. In the first of these, "Ceremony," one partner, whom I take to be the husband, waits only four lines to start in on "One thing I've always hated / about you: I hate that you refuse / to have people at the house." He accuses her of isolation, the same quality Telemachus finds in Penelope, and of refusal (the enjambment makes "refuse" an intransitive as well as transitive verb) as a pervasive habit of emotion. He complains of the "boarding school" rigidity of her meals, "chicken Monday, fish Tuesday." She replies,

"Why do you call it rigidity? / Can't you call it a taste / for ceremony?" which suggests that what Telemachus calls "the child's / hunger for ritual," as a way to "address / that sense of being / insufficiently loved" lingers in her still. If the roles of spouse and parent are difficult, that is because they require one to relinquish the habitual role of slighted child. Within such limits, her husband says, there can be "Pleasure maybe but not / joy." Their relationship, like that of Penelope and Odysseus, depends on a ritual of avoidance, a refusal to be fully present for and to each other.

In the last exchange, "Heart's Desire," which is also the last poem of the book, the reclusive woman who "hate[s] parties" nonetheless wants to have one, complete with "meat from Lobel's." The giving and receiving of food, as usual in Glück's work, stands as the metaphor of emotional exchange. She imagines a gathering that includes all, or almost all, heart's desires present and past, "all my old lovers. / Maybe even your ex-girlfriends, except / the exhibitionists." The mordantly witty exception registers her abiding hurt and suspicion even in this expansive moment, and her husband is skeptical: "If I were you, / I'd start with the meat order." She wants to move beyond pleasure to joy at last: "When you look into people's faces / you'll see how happy they are. / Some are dancing, maybe. . . ." Again, his voice is the bell tolling her back to her usual withheld and withholding self: "The point isn't whether or not / the guests are happy. / The point is whether or not / they're dead." He knows that in the world they have built together, happiness, dancing, and emotional abandon are inevitably the primrose path to ruin. "Trust me," she answers, "no one's / going to be hurt again," as if conceding the point that in the past someone always was. "For one night, affection / will triumph over passion. The passion / will all be in the music." Passion has always been a destroyer, and therefore one goes beyond pleasure to joy at one's own peril. But passion can be sublimated into the music, allowing affection to triumph. There is still an ambivalence toward passion, an insistence that it needs to be defeated, even as it is given its displaced due. In this book more than in others, Glück succeeds in making myth and quotidian experience illuminate each other. She shows us how much stifled rage there must have been in the familial relations among Penelope, Odysseus, and Telemachus, but also how much misgiving loyalty and furtive love hide beneath the bickering of her modern couple.

IV. "Yet Why Not Say What Happened?": *Ararat*

My favorites among Glück's collections are *Ararat* and *The Wild Iris,* which seem to mark polarities of her imagination. *The Wild Iris* (1992), with flowers that address the gardener much as the gardener addresses an unresponsive God, with its steady movement from the first stirrings of spring to the end of autumn, translates the personal into natural metaphors, framing it within the macrocosm in a more telling way than the mythological poems, even at their best, can do. In contrast, *Ararat* (1990) is the most unabashedly autobiographical of her books since *Firstborn,* but with a technical mastery and restraint gained in the twenty-two years between. In it, she seems to have arrived at a position like Robert Lowell's in the late poem "Epilogue"; though he may "want to make / something imagined, not recalled," the poet finally stops resisting and asks: "Yet why not say what happened?" *Ararat* is the book in which Glück comes closest to narrating what happened.

The title *Ararat* turns out to refer to the cemetery, Mount Ararat, where the poet's dead sister is buried, but both cemetery and book are named, of course, for the mountain where Noah's ark came to rest after forty days on the annihilating flood, sheltering its biological minimum of two survivors per species. So the title prepares us for a voyage of survival amid destruction, and for a consideration of what, minimally, will suffice; also for questions of how to reconstitute a world that has been catastrophically shattered.

The first line of *Ararat*'s first poem, "*Parodos,*" also begins its last poem, "First Memory": "Long ago, I was wounded." The presence of the word "First" in the title of the closing poem, along with its return to the opening words of the book, suggests a backward quest for a wholeness prior to the wound, as the epigraph from Plato confirms: "human nature was originally one and we were a whole, and the desire and pursuit of the whole is called love" [*eros*]. Freud, in *Beyond the Pleasure Principle,* proposed that one "universal attribute of instincts" is "*an urge inherent in organic life to restore an earlier state of things* which the living entity has been obliged to abandon under the pressure of external disturbing forces."[17] If we accept this hypothesis, "we shall be compelled to say that '*the aim of all life is death,*' and, looking backwards, that '*inanimate things existed before living ones*'" (32, his emphasis). For this reason, Freud posits a death instinct, *thanatos,* coexisting in tension with *eros.* For Glück, the encounter with *thanatos* is primary, a necessary precondition of the acknowledgment (and perhaps even the experience) of *eros*.[18]

In the *Symposium,* erotic desire arises from the attempt to re-unite the sexes, who were once copresent in one whole body. Sexual difference is the originary wound that heterosexual desire yearns to heal. But in "*Parodos,*" Glück's first response to the un-specified wound of long ago is thanatic: she seeks to become as much like inanimate matter as a sentient human being can:

> I'll tell you
> what I meant to be—
> a device that listened.
> Not inert: still.
> A piece of wood. A stone.

In the closing stanza, she describes her "vocation" (a bit too por-tentously, but it's one of a very few weak moments in an extraor-dinary book) as bearing "witness / to the great mysteries," which she names as "birth and death."

From the outset, beginnings and endings, procreation and death, appear together. The difficulty of distinguishing these contraries emerges strikingly in the second poem, "A Fantasy." "I'll tell you something:" the poem begins, "every day / people are dying. And that's just the beginning." Each death is also a birth, as "new wid-ows are born, / new orphans," who must now "decide about this new life" they have suddenly entered. The widow cannot yet ac-cept the new life that her loss inaugurates:

> She wants to be back in the cemetery,
> back in the sickroom, the hospital. She knows
> it isn't possible. But it's her only hope,
> the wish to move backward. And just a little,
> not so far as the marriage, the first kiss.

"*An urge inherent in organic life to restore an earlier state of things* which the living entity has been obliged to abandon under the pressure of external disturbing forces," said Freud. Here, the earlier state is the time, so fresh in memory yet irrevocably far, when her husband was still alive. So the urge to go backward attempts to recover the union of husband and wife, the couple joined by *eros,* but the drive to go backward ends in death, the reunion with the inanimate. Perhaps sensing not only the impossibility but the ultimate nihilism of the "wish to move backward," the widow wants to go backward "just a little." To go all the way back to the first kiss would be to undo the intervening years of life together. And having gone back so far, could one stop there?

In the next four poems, we learn that the death in "A Fantasy" is not a hypothetical instance, but the beginning of an autobiographical account of Glück's response—and that of her mother, sisters, and aunt—to the death of her father, which in turn is shadowed by other deaths, most notably the death in infancy of one of Glück's sisters. But the wound of long ago was prior to all of these. The father's death both repeats that primal injury (one of emotional abandonment, as death is a physical abandonment), and changes the poet's relationship to it, initiating a backward-looking quest to understand and accept, if not heal, the wounded state that has been virtually a lifelong condition.

The survivors are all women, a wife and two daughters. "A Novel" suggests that with the father's death, the impetus forward in time that drives a novel's plot has disappeared for them, since "In this house, when you say *plot* what you mean is *love story*." Though the father provided only a "weak" version of "the hero," a "figurehead," he was nonetheless "needed," and without him there is no love story, no *eros*-generating plot. On the first anniversary of the death, time remains as inert as it had in the first shock of loss. Only the sister's small daughter "wants . . . / to make time pass." But to "the rest," adults with a longer perspective, "a whole lifetime is nothing." From early childhood to the deathbed is "Not a sentence, but a breath, a caesura." There is no time to construct meaning, which must unfold as a sentence, or even to make poetry about the brevity of life, since the poetic line is cut short at the caesura. Or, to read the metaphor more strictly: life is the pause in a line that was being spoken before birth and continues after death, a brief interruption of the poem of nonbeing.

The father, though dead, is nonetheless repeated and perpetuated in the psyches of the survivors. They place no flowers on his grave but instead plant flowers in the garden of the house, which the mother and sister "both see / . . . as his true grave." There is no separation between house and grave, living and dead. Moreover, as we see later in the book, the father himself tried to minimize the separation between life and death:

> What he wanted
> was to lie on the couch
> with the *Times*
> over his face,
> so that death, when it came,
> wouldn't seem a significant change.
>
> —"New World"

The poet behaves in the same spirit when she seeks to become a piece of wood or a stone, and the sister also carries on the tradition through her response to the destruction, in a storm, of the poppies she has planted but has not seen in bloom:

> That means
> she's going to feel deprived again.
>
> But for my sister, that's the condition of love.
> She was my father's daughter:
> the face of love, to her,
> is the face turning away.
>
> —"Love of Flowers"

One can only love what has turned away, and one can only repeat the gesture and turn away in order to avoid being hurt anew. The immobilization of desire is finally a defense against the thwarting of desire, as the poet admits in her "Confession":

> Like anyone, I have my dreams.
> But I've learned to hide them,
> to protect myself
> from fulfillment: all happiness
> attracts the Fates' anger.

But immobility, as the sequence moves forward, begins to betray its inadequacy, its masking of turbulent panic. Reflecting on her mother's attempts to soothe her dying husband as she had once tried to soothe her dying infant, Glück remarks that "The dying are like tops, like gyroscopes— / they spin so rapidly they seem to be still. / Then they fly apart: . . ." ("Lullaby"). One can long to be inert, like matter, but even matter is not inert. It is volatile like the human spirit: "The soul's like all matter: / why would it stay intact, stay faithful to its one form, / when it could be free?" The primal integrity, when in Plato's words "human nature was . . . one and we were whole," is unstable, bound to fall apart, setting in motion the desire that struggles to recover it.

Other irreconcilable dualisms seem to emerge out of the underlying antithesis of whole and wounded. If the dead and the living sister make one pair of opposites, the poet and the living sister make another. "Appearances" contrasts the "two who lived" as they appear in portraits done when the poet was seven years old: "I'm the dark one, the older one. My sister's blond, / the one who looks angry because she can't talk. // It never bothered me, not talking." One is darkness and silence, the other light and volubility. And, as she later observes in "Yellow Dahlia," it is hard to avoid the idea that "If there are two things / then one must be better." The mother, though aware of the contrast, "tried to love us equally" and hung the two portraits so that the children seemed to face one another. But despite her efforts, "anytime she ministered to one child, loved that child, / she damaged the other." Her denial of that unavoidable choice, however, is necessary to prevent yet another sundering, for "Without that, she'd have been torn apart." "[Y]ou had to shut out / one child to see the other," the poet insists, and then, as if in expiation of guilt at her own bitterness, depicts herself in the next poem as "The Untrustworthy Speaker," the one who must be shut out:

> If you want the truth, you have to close yourself
> to the older daughter, block her out:
> when a living being is hurt like that
> in its deepest workings,
> all function is altered.

The suffering of early trauma does not ennoble character but deforms it: "we're the cripples, the liars; / we're the ones who should be factored out / in the interest of truth." The poem leaves us with a conundrum rather like the Cretan Liar Paradox: if an unreliable speaker says she is unreliable, should we believe her? She says she has "learned to hear like a psychiatrist," to become the "device that listened" that she aspired to be in "*Parodos,*" but might that not be the very habit that makes her unreliable: her insistence that she is separate from what she hears, that there is a part of her that somehow knows, objectively, that she cannot "see anything objectively"? What if this tactic itself generates the untrustworthiness?

Once again she turns on herself in "A Fable," which twists the story of Solomon's judgment. Instead of two mothers claiming the same child, here are two sisters claiming the same mother. Just as it is the mother's willingness to renounce her claim in order to spare the child that reveals her to Solomon, here the daughter who is "willing to destroy / [her]self" imagines she will be recognized as "the rightful child, / the one who couldn't bear / to divide the mother." But this tale is a fable not of justice, but of unconscious childhood fantasy. If we read the previous poem's self-accusation as a form of self-destruction, it begins to look like a literalization of the fantasy diagnosed in this sequel. Self-abnegation will not make the mother choose one sister over the other, nor can it lead to a "reliable" sense of one's own identity.

In "Brown Circle," the poet compares her relationship with her son to her own relationship with her mother and finds that her much-sought disinterestedness can become only another version of "the face turning away," the inability to engage emotionally with those one loves. She finds herself unable to "love [her] son / the way [she]'d meant to love him"; instead,

> What I am
> is the scientist,
> who comes to that flower
> with a magnifying glass
> and doesn't leave, though
> the sun burns a brown
> circle of grass around
> the flower. Which is
> more or less the way
> my mother loved me.

Here, the lens refracts more heat than light. The urge to examine dispassionately, long ago adopted as a defense against one's own vulnerability, burns its object, which is not inert matter but another living, vulnerable being. Dispassion may seem kinder than anger, but it repeats the pattern of the parents, who "couldn't bring themselves / to inflict pain" and instead "preferred / tribunals" ("Animals"). That approach has produced children like the poet and her sister, who both conclude that "the best way / to love us was not to / spend time with us"; again, love is only possible when its expression is withheld or thwarted; the face that turns away, not the face that sees you, is the one that loves you.

By the time we reach "Snow," the figure of love as the averted gaze has acquired force enough to freight a familiar image with disturbing implications. A father carrying his daughter on his shoulders might seem an almost sentimental emblem of paternal affection, but not here:

> My father liked
> to stand like this, to hold me
> so he couldn't see me.
> I remember
> staring straight ahead
> into the world my father saw; . . .

By keeping his daughter out of sight, the father teaches her to do the same with those she loves. She is staring into the world her father sees not only because she looks from the same vantage point, but because in the very act of holding her in this way, he is teaching her to see as he sees.

Two poems near the end of the book drive it toward closure. In "Paradise," we get a glimpse of what the first wound of "long ago" was. She sees the place she grew up in, which has gone from "village" to "almost a city," as a lost Eden, and claims that her sister cannot "know what it once was." In the last stanza, she sees herself not as Eve, but as "Adam, / . . . the firstborn":

> Believe me, you never heal,
> you never forget the ache in your side,
> the place where something was taken away
> to make another person.

The primal wound, like Sartre's hell, would seem to be other people, the loss of the solipsism of infancy. Juxtaposing her allusion with the original story, we may take it that from this loss comes knowledge, guilt, and desire. This poem also resonates with the epigraph from Plato, since Eve was once part of Adam's flesh, as the two sexes were supposedly once united in a single body. The notion that the other is made by taking something away from oneself implies that in the beginning there was only one, self-sufficient body, and that other bodies cannot exist independently, but only as subtraction from and division of the primal whole. (Not to need other bodies would be one solution to the problem of autonomy represented, in *Descending Figure,* through the metaphor of anorexia nervosa.)

The other pivotal poem is "Mirror Image," in which the daughter's perpetuation of her father, implied at many points earlier, becomes explicit:

> Tonight I saw myself in the dark window as
> the image of my father, whose life
> was spent like this,
> thinking of death, to the exclusion
> of other sensual matters,
> so in the end that life
> was easy to give up, . . .

"[L]ike this" points to the moment of writing that produces the poem, as if to confess that making poetry so obsessed with death and loss is not entirely different from the father's routine of lying on the couch with the *Times* over his face. Not even the mother's entreaties could make him "turn back" from dying, since "he believed / that once you can't love another human being / you have no place in the world." Now the epigraph appears in a different light: "the desire and pursuit of the whole is called love," but the pursuit can lead either toward union with another human being, which attempts to restore the wholeness of undivided "human nature," not yet split into male and female, I and thou. Or it can lead toward a rejection of all particular attachments, as in Shelley's "Die, / If thou wouldst be with that which thou dost seek!" (*Adonais*).

The closing poem, "First Memory," adds one more turn to Glück's dialectic of *eros* and *thanatos.* Considering once more the wound of "long ago" and its damage to "what I was," the speaker recognizes that

> from the beginning of time,
> in childhood, I thought
> that pain meant
> I was not loved.
> It meant I loved.

To consider "the beginning of time" coeval with one's own birth is to place Shelley's "white radiance of eternity" out of bounds. For better or for worse, subjectivity begins and ends within the many-colored dome, and love must find its objects there, if anywhere at all. Having always attributed "pain" to rejection, principally by her father, against whom she has sought "revenge," she realizes that the agent of her suffering is not some other who has denied her love. For that denial would not matter if she were indifferent to the face turning away. She has suffered because she continues to love and therefore remains vulnerable to rejection. The attempt, described in "*Parodos,*" to achieve the insensibility of wood or stone has been an attempt to deny that she loves, to become both invulnerable and separate from her interaction with others. The last line stops short of renouncing the project of detachment; it says that pain is the result of love but does not rule on whether love with its attendant pain is preferable to a life free of either emotion—if indeed such a life is possible.

V. What the Flowers Tell Me: *The Wild Iris*

As Helen Vendler observes, in *Ararat* Glück "turned away from symbol to 'real life,'" describing it with a ruthless flatness, then "reversing course" in *The Wild Iris* to write "a very opulent, symbolic book."[19] Through the monologues of the speaking flowers, juxtaposed with the gardener's repeated prayers at "Matins" and "Vespers" and the replies of her caustic god (lowercase throughout the volume), Glück builds a sustained analogy, concisely described by Vendler: "As the flowers are to their gardener-poet, so she is to her gardener-god; the flowers, in their stoic biological collectivity, and their pathos, speak to her, sometimes reproachfully, as she speaks, imploringly, to her god" (*Soul Says,* 17). As Vendler reminds us by comparisons to Herbert and Dickinson, Glück alludes to a long tradition when she invokes flowers as emblems of the soul (*Soul Says,* 17–18). *The Wild Iris* gains further coherence by following the progression of time, from the earliest spring to the deaths of the last flowers in autumn, just as the prayers shift, after the pivotal arrival of "Midsummer"—first mentioned in "Heaven and Earth," situated on page 32, at the exact middle of the 63-page sequence—from "Matins" to "Vespers." In so doing, it dramatizes the conflict between linear and cyclical conceptions of time. Almost all of Glück's flowers are perennials;[20] the tension lies in the relationship between the individual flower and the dormant bulb or root that will regenerate next spring. In which of these does the human spirit recognize its own condition?

The first poem speaks through the wild iris, under whose sign the whole sequence unfolds. It begins with a clarion affirmation of cyclical return:

> At the end of my suffering
> there was a door.
>
> Hear me out: that which you call death
> I remember.
>
> —"The Wild Iris"

To remember death is to know it is not final; the iris, like Plato's man of Er, has not been dipped in the river of forgetfulness. Although "It is terrible to survive / as consciousness / buried in the dark earth," this state of "being / a soul and unable / to speak" eventually ends. The alert reader of Glück will notice a similarity between the iris in its buried, dormant state and the speaker of "*Parodos*" in *Ararat,* who wanted to be "a device that listened. / Not inert: still. / A piece of wood. A stone." The dreaded condition is not only literal death, but the painful death-in-life already deeply explored in Glück's work. The iris insists that "whatever / returns from oblivion returns / to find a voice," as the poet herself has had to emerge from wood- or stone-like silence in order to speak as well as listen. As Vendler points out, the bulb underground is already, for Herbert and Dickinson, an image of "spiritual deprivation" (*Soul Says,* 17), but in the context of Glück's other poems, we can recognize her individual mode of spiritual deprivation in the flower's language.[21] The powerful closing lines of "The Wild Iris" also stir echoes from other poems: "from the center of my life came / a great fountain, deep blue / shadows on azure seawater." The first two of these lines seem overwhelmingly affirmative, reminiscent of Rilke's giving fountain-mouth (*Sonette an Orpheus* II.xv), its "deep blue" the sustaining water of life. But then "blue" turns out to be an adjective modifying "shadow"—is the iris then a shadow-fountain, pouring out empty forms, illusions of immortality? The azure seawater recalls "the waters, blue and permanent," in "The Drowned Children," no longer landlocked, but illimitable. And seawater is full of salt; we cannot drink it.

From the very first poem, then, Glück has undermined her own analogy of human and floral life with an implied skepticism. We should not be entirely surprised, then, when the voice of the "Re-treating Wind"—god as *spiritus,* who first breathed life into Adam's clay—warns his human creatures: "Whatever you hoped, / you will not find yourselves in the garden, / among the growing plants. / Your lives are not circular like theirs." Already, in "End of Winter," we've been told that in the emerging world of spring and summer (which in the seasonal metaphor is the time of living, as autumn and winter are the time of death), we will not hear the divine voice clearly, but "only / persistent echoing / in all sound that means good-bye, good-bye— / the one continuous line / that binds us to each other." There is return in the sense of the echo, the persistence of the past in the present, but time is a "continuous line," not a circle, and we are bound to each other not only in the sense of con-soling connection but of common mortality also. The line, like a chain, "binds us" as prisoners.

In the second pair of "Matins," the gardener tries to make anal-ogies between the plants and god, rather than between plants and god's other creations. She "cannot love / what [she] can't conceive," but since god will "disclose / virtually nothing," conception requires analogy. With so little to go on, analogy can be provisional at best: is god "like the hawthorn tree, / always the same thing in the same place," or "more the foxglove, inconsistent"? God's "silence that pro-motes belief / [he] must be all things," foxglove, hawthorn, also rose, daisy and the rest, has the opposite result: that which could be any-thing must be nothing, so "we are left to think / you couldn't pos-sibly exist." Or perhaps he intends us to think he does not exist; the first "Matins" ends with a catalogue of absences: "the silence of the morning, / the crickets not yet rubbing their wings, the cats / not fighting in the yard." Maybe it is dormancy and absence, the bulb rather than the flourishing plant, that most nearly resembles god. But this precarious negative theology cannot satisfy the speaker of the second "Matins," who cannot accept "the absence / of all feeling, of the least / concern for me."[22] She has begun by likening god to the birch trees, who must not be addressed "in the personal way," and ends by daring the birches to "do their worst, let them / bury me with the Romantics. . . ." For Glück, the Romantics represent a se-ductive but dangerous possibility of her own poetic temperament, much as Stevens invoked them as singers of "unreal songs" ("Cre-dences of Summer"), too ready to "bethou" each thing in nature, to hear a voice where there is only "[a] sound like any other" that "will end" ("Notes Toward a Supreme Fiction").

The self-pitying fantasy of burial draws a sharp rebuke not from a single flower, but from an entire patch of scilla: "Not I, you idiot, not self, but we, we—waves / of sky blue like / a critique of heaven" ("Scilla"). Vendler reads this passage as urging the poet "to abandon herself to collective biological being" (*Soul Says,* 18); one might also read it as the siren song of postmodern critiques not only "of heaven" as telos of the perfected individual soul, but of the belief in coherent, autonomous selfhood, to which Glück's poetics is so strongly committed. The blue that in the iris came "from the center of [its] life" reappears, moving now in sourceless waves. We recall, also, that in the first "Matins," Noah tells her that it "is an error of depressives, identifying / with a tree," because "the happy heart / wanders the garden like a falling leaf, a figure for / the part, not the whole." Plato's *Symposium* notwithstanding, "the desire and pursuit of the whole" may not be the best way to live.

The first garden, Eden, had not one gardener but two, the primal couple, Adam and Eve. The four poems following "Retreating Wind" reveal that the gardener-poet has a male companion, and that all is not well between them. The first of these, "The Garden," observes a "young couple" (who may be the speaker and her man as they once were) planting "a row of peas, as though / no one has ever done this before." Even at this early stage, there is tension between them, as "She wants to stop; / he wants to get to the end, . . ." When she touches his face, it seems less a gesture of love than of "truce," and "even here, even at the beginning of love, / her hand leaving his face makes / an image of departure." In "The Hawthorn Tree," the gardener addresses someone walking next to her, "Side by side, not / hand in hand"; this couple is long past the hand-holding stage. Her companion has withdrawn from her, and she can infer "the cause of [his] flight, human / passion or rage," from the fact that he has "let drop" the flowers he has been gathering. "Love in Moonlight" opens by throwing a vat of cold water on its romantic title:

> Sometimes a man or woman forces his despair
> on another person, which is called
> baring the heart, alternatively, baring the soul—
> meaning for this moment they acquired souls—

What is taken for love, then, is a gesture of despair in which someone tries to persuade himself and the other party that both have souls after all, and are not mere creatures of fear and appetite. It is, as the closing lines suggest, like the reflected light of the moon, a lovely appearance "taken / from another source" and therefore neither self-sustaining nor trustworthy. If this likeness between love and moonlight proves that "stone or not, / the moon is still that much of a living thing," the converse is also true: the illusion of love can shine on the most barren stone.

The group of love poems ends with "April," in which the chastising god sees the couple showing their mutual anger through "tiresome outward signs; the man / pointedly weeding an entire forest, / the woman limping, refusing to change clothes / or wash her hair," and catches them thinking *No one's despair is like my despair*—a variation on Jeremiah's "Behold, and see if there be any sorrow like unto my sorrow" (Lamentations 1:7), but also recalling the despair that one person forces on another. Again, Glück turns on her own desire that one's sufferings should prove to be unique signs of election; rather, "grief is distributed / between you, among all your kind, for me / to know you, as deep blue / marks the wild scilla. . . ." It is our common color, not welling up from the center of an individual life, as the iris would have it, but the mode in which all people, men and women alike, must live. As for the desperate baring of the soul in order to acquire a soul to bare, the violets, in the next poem, remind their "poor sad god" that "either you never have one / or you never lose one" ("Violets"). By the end of the sequence, the man appears to have abandoned the woman: "Love of my life, you / are lost," she laments, in a poem ("Vespers: *Parousia*") whose object of address is ambiguously poised between earthly lover and absent god.

After another interlude of Matins prayers, the flowers continue their derisive critique of the human project of spiritual transcendence. Longing for "eternal life," people "don't look at" or "listen to" the flowers at their feet, preferring to shake the

> little rattle—O
> the soul! the soul! Is it enough
> only to look inward? Contempt
> for humanity is one thing, but why
> disdain the expansive
> field, your gaze rising over the clear heads
> of the wild buttercups into what?
> —"Field Flowers"

"[T]he expansive / field" recalls that most un-Glückian poet, Charles Olson, who thought of poetic composition as the movement of attention through a field of objects and forces, and who urged "getting rid of the lyrical interference of the individual as ego" ("Projective Verse"). The heads of the buttercups are clear, those of the humans muddled with self-preoccupation. In "The Red Poppy," another flower suggests still another alternative to the closed, inward-directed gaze. To abandon "mind" for "feelings," as the poppy does, might seem only another form of solipsism, except that the feeling is directed outward: "I have / a lord in heaven / called the sun, and open / for him, showing him / the fire of my own heart, fire / like his presence." This openness, at once erotic and religious, asks no questions. Flower and sun share the common element of "fire" and partake of each other's nature. The poppy asks its "brothers and sisters" if they once had resembled it, "long ago, / before you were human? Did you / permit yourselves / to open once, who would never / open again?" Or perhaps, one might speculate, after we were human but before we stopped believing in an unquestionable bond between "a lord in heaven" and ourselves. This poem reminds me of Larkin's "Solar," which Seamus Heaney praises for its unexpected "generosity," its opening of "stops that [Larkin] usually keeps muted."[23] "The Red Poppy" is also uncharacteristic of Glück in its affirmation of emotional openness and "fire"; in "Lamium," Glück places herself among those who believe they "live for truth and, by extension, love / all that is cold." And it must be balanced—as Heaney says "Solar" must be balanced against "Sad Steps"—against other poems,[24] such as "Spring Snow," which suggests that the poppy's glad submission answers a "demand" born of weakness: "I have shown you what you want: / not belief, but capitulation / to authority, which depends on violence." Here, what looked like emotional generosity in "The Red Poppy" looks like loss of autonomy, blind submission to power.

The sequence pivots on a group of three poems, "Heaven and Earth," "The Doorway," and "Midsummer." These mark the point of greatest fullness, between "the extremes" (heaven and earth, birth and death, spring and fall), which are comparatively "easy" in their starkness: "Only / the middle is a puzzle. Midsummer— / everything is possible. // Meaning: never again will life end" ("Heaven and Earth"). Of course it will, but for the time being one cannot conceive of limitation. "John," the speaker's son, "stands at the horizon," in the open possibility of childhood; "he wants / both at once, he wants / everything at once." Not only the child, but the wife and husband are "dreaming this sort of thing," and subjective time stops "as the fire of the summer sun / truly does stall / being entirely contained by / the burning maples / at the garden's border." Here the unbanked fire of "The Red Poppy" is "contained," enclosed like the garden itself by the maples. For once, time and permanence, energy and form, seem reconciled, but we remember that to stall is only to delay, and that the maple leaves, taking the sun's fire into themselves, will turn and fall.

The title of "The Doorway" recalls the iris's opening declaration that "a door" waits at the end of its suffering in the earth. In this poem, the speaker wishes to linger at the threshold: "not in midsummer but the moment before / the first flower forms, the moment / nothing is as yet past." Despite the midsummer illusion that "never again will life end," to move from nascency to being is to take the first step toward death: as soon as the flower "forms," it has a body in the world, vulnerable to time and accident. In this mood, she is prepared "to succumb / to nothing"—which may be taken as invincibility or submission to nothingness as a way of avoiding the terrors of being. It is a time "before the appearance of the gift, / before possession." "Possession," like "nothing," has a double sense: it is both possession *of* the world and its fullness and helpless possession *by* that world. In "Midsummer," the god-voice surveys the field, in which the formed flowers, already in "possession," "all want / different things—sunlight and shadow, / moist darkness, dry heat." They persist in believing, Platonically, that "something could fuse [them] into a whole." Plato called that desire for wholeness love, but Glück's embittered god sees in it the root of strife:

> each calling out
> some need, some absolute
>
> and in that name continually
> strangling each other
> in the open field—
>
> For what? For space and air?
> The privilege of being
> single in the eyes of heaven?

When the desire for god to intervene and fuse everything into a whole is frustrated, each created being in desperation asserts its own nature as an "absolute" and demands that all others be either absorbed in it or killed. If we may not all be as one, then let me at least be single under the eye of heaven. Here, god sides with the scilla in rejecting the claims of singularity: "You were not intended / to be unique. You were / my embodiment, all diversity." The gardener, in the last of the ensuing group of three "Vespers," wonders whether god loves "the beasts of the field, even, / possibly, the field itself" more than herself and his other human creatures.

As the sequence moves past meridian, from "Matins" to "Vespers," god, speaking in "End of Summer," considers loving nothing at all: "After all things occurred to me, / the void occurred to me." In the beginning, the earth was without form and void, says Genesis, and now, with creation's summer ending, god says: "There is a limit / to the pleasure I had in form. . . ." The created beings are "too little like [him] in the end / to please [him]." In this gnostic mood, he asks the poet to see him as "the emptiness of heaven / mirrored on earth" in the approaching winter snow, where "white light" is "no longer disguised as matter." Having built Shelley's dome of many-colored glass, he is ready to smash it. In "Harvest," he speaks of creation and destruction as cyclical, meant to point a lesson:

> how many times must I destroy my own creation
> to teach you
> this is your punishment:
>
> with one gesture I established you
> in time and in paradise.

For us, there can be no experience of paradise that is not also subject to time. The fire of the sun may stall in the maples, and we are capable of feeling that never again will life end, but the moment passes, the sun sets, we age and die. God's words here revise the account in Genesis, which tells us that death and generation came only after the fall. In Glück's version, Adam and Eve were already in time, bound by cycles of creation and destruction, from the first gesture of their creation.

Toward the end of the book, the flowers speak in knowledge of their impending deaths. The ipomoea, or morning glory vine, is an isolated annual in the garden of perennials, full of "sorrow, that I am not to be / permitted to ascend ever again, / never in any sense / permitted to repeat my life" ("Ipomoea"). It asks god why he has "drawn from" it "flowers like the sky, except / to mark me as a part / of my master." The only consolation the ipomoea can muster is the one god urges in "Spring Snow": the "capitulation / to authority." In the "Vespers" that follows, the poet is almost as despairing as the flower. She surmises that god has taught her "to love the world, making it impossible / to turn away completely" despite her knowledge that he "mean[s] to take it away," so that she will be "so starved for hope" she will "refuse to see that finally / nothing was left to [her], and would believe instead / in the end you [god] were left to [her]." But if turning away completely were possible, it is apparently the course she would choose. God's cruel strategy of starving her for hope (the phrase returns us to the theme of ontological hunger so prominent in *Descending Figure*) leaves her asking, in another "Vespers" prayer, "In what contempt do you hold us / to believe only loss can impress / your power on us[?]"

The closing poems of the sequence engage not only the finality of life, but its refusal to yield an intelligible meaning. God has already warned, in "Retreating Light," that he is "tired of telling stories," leaving us to tell them for ourselves. But the only plotline we can imagine ends in our obliteration; better not to "spend too much time looking ahead" ("Vespers"), but rather to accept that one "can flourish, having / no hope / of enduring." Maybe the red poppy is right after all. God, however, would provide a meaning if he could. "My sorrow," he says, "[is] that I cannot answer you / in speech you accept as mine" ("Sunset"). Lacking any "faith in [our] own language" either, we "invest / authority in signs / [we] cannot read with any accuracy." "My tenderness," he concludes, "should be apparent to you / in the breeze of the summer evening / and in the words that become / your own response." In this last line, god claims that the very power of response evident in our own words is the best evidence of his goodwill. That the words are ours and not his does not mean that they do not reveal him.

If Glück had ended the book with "Sunset," we might be left with a sense of unwarranted optimism, but the last of god's addresses to his creatures strikes a more somber note. He calls the living world a "chaos," rather than an ordered cosmos, and says he is "tired of" it. He reminds us that we "come and go; eventually / I forget your names" ("September Twilight"). So much for the believer's hope of being written into the Book of Life for all eternity. Rather, we shall be erased like "a draft to be thrown away." The analogy underpinning the sequence now acquires an additional set of terms, implicit before but only now brought forward: god is to the creation as gardener is to flowers, and as poet is to poem. When god says "I've finished you, vision / of deepest mourning," he announces the impending end of the book, Glück's own vision of deepest mourning, as well. And, as so often before, the verb has an ominous multiple sense: "finish" means to complete, to bring to perfection, and also to put an end to, to exhaust or destroy. At least from the human vantage point, god appears not to see, any more than the gardener recognizes the "child's terror" of the gold lily ("The Gold Lily"). The flower begs the gardener, "you who raised me," to save it and its dying "companions," as a child begs a parent for protection. But the man and woman who made the garden are also helpless and frightened: "the evening turns / cold with their terror" ("The White Lilies"). The affirmative note of the book's close is powerful because it so fully acknowledges the pressure of mortality:

> Hush, beloved. It doesn't matter to me
> how many summers I live to return:
> this one summer we have entered eternity.
> I felt your two hands
> bury me to release its splendor.

The gardener accepts the lesson god teaches in "Harvest," that we are "established" in eternity and time at once, with no choice but to suffer their radical disjunction. In the last two lines, the speaker takes on faith that her burial—her suffering, her abandonment— has been visited on her in order to bring forth the splendor of eternity, as one buries a bulb in order to bring forth a flower.

The Wild Iris, like all of Glück's volumes, is a somber book, but more than any of the others, it includes the evocation of plenitude along with mourning for its inevitable loss. Even here, Glück's world is narrowly circumscribed, if rich within its boundaries: it is the garden, the house, the restless couple and their child. In my attempt to triangulate her position by analogies to Blake, Wordsworth, Shelley, Stevens, and Celan, I can't help feeling that a small excellence has been set too nearly level with larger ones. For god's plenty, we must continue to look elsewhere. But in *The Wild Iris,* Glück allows the Prolific to answer the Devouring, and stages their conflict more evenhandedly than usual. For that reason, it strikes me as the most capacious and generous volume of her poems to date.[25]

1. David V. Erdman, ed., *The Poetry and Prose of William Blake,* commentary by Harold Bloom (Garden City: Doubleday, 1965) 39.

2. See, for instance, Lee Upton, *The Muse of Abandonment: Origin, Identity, Mastery in Five American Poets* (Lewisburg: Bucknell University Press/London: Associated University Presses, 1988): "In her second book, *The House on Marshland* (1975), Glück . . . has exorcised the revulsions of *Firstborn* in favor of . . . more conscious awareness" (127); Elizabeth Dodd, *The Veiled Mirror and the Woman Poet: H. D., Louise Bogan, Elizabeth Bishop, and Louise Glück* (Columbia: University of Missouri Press, 1992): "Glück is clearly leaving behind her early debt to the language of the confessionals" (159); Helen Vendler, *Part of Nature, Part of Us:* "The leap in style from Glück's relatively unformed first book . . . to *The House on Marshland* suggests that she is her own best critic" (311). Most tellingly, there is Glück herself, who during her 1993 baccalaureate address at Williams College presented "La Force," "the last poem added to that manuscript, not because it is good but because it begins a narrative. It is a poem I would never otherwise read aloud" (*Proofs & Theories,* 130).

3. Calvin Bedient, "Birth, Not Death, Is the Hard Loss," *Parnassus* 9, no. 1 (1981): 168.

4. In *The Triumph of Achilles,* "Brooding Likeness" begins with the statement, "I was born in the month of the bull"; Taurus is also Glück's birth sign, although the earlier poem drops no hint of that.

5. Wallace Stevens, "Credences of Summer, II." Vendler, in *Part of Nature, Part of Us,* makes passing comparisons of Glück's poems to those of both Stevens and Keats (not surprising, to be sure, since Vendler's own work has engaged so deeply with both).

6. "It is hard to know how to begin talking about something which is so badly written or so confusedly written or so morally slack or so portentous and pretentious and so foolish and so unfeeling." See Greg Kuzma, "Rock Bottom: Louise Glück and the Poetry of Dispassion," *Midwest Quarterly* 24 (summer 1983): 471.

7. "Adonais," 39; "When Lilacs Last in the Dooryard Bloom'd," 14; and *In Memoriam,* 130, respectively.

8. But I am struck with the parallel to a remark in Ludwig Binswanger's "The Case of Ellen West," in which his anorexic patient confides: "Even as a child she thinks it 'interesting' to have a fatal accident—for example, to break through the ice while skating." See "The Case of Ellen West" (1944), trans. Werner M. Mendel and Joseph Lyons, in *Existence: A New Dimension in Psychiatry and Psychology,* ed. Rollo May, Ernest Angel, and Henri F. Ellenberger (New York: Basic Books, 1958) 283. This case history is, of course, a source for Frank Bidart, the other poet who has written memorably about anorexia nervosa. Since Glück considers Bidart "one of the crucial figures of our time, and, very likely, a major poet" (*Proofs & Theories,* 59), it seems likely that she has read not only his "Ellen West" but also the Binswanger case history, which is explicitly cited as the poem's source on the acknowledgments page of *The Book of the Body.*

Reading "The Drowned Children" in the context of this case history and of Glück's own poems about anorexia prompts a speculation that something of the child's compulsion to drown remains in the adult anorexic's psyche. Subsequent references to Binswanger will appear in the text.

9. Kuzma objects to the imprecise use of this metaphor: "when she talks about them 'slipping over the pond' I must say I've never seen any that do that" (477). This objection seems to me more telling than the moral one; I shall return to the curious sliding of Glück's metaphors later in the essay. At times I find this instability merely careless, but at others it has, in Hart Crane's phrase, an internal "logic of metaphor."

10. Dodd, *The Veiled Mirror*, 187. Subsequent references will appear in the text.

11. These lines leave open whether the child is hurt by the father's coldness (not being touched) or by an implicit threat of abuse. Elizabeth Dodd notes, in *The Veiled Mirror,* that "the touching the little girl does not receive from her father may simply be parental affection" (18), while Mary Kinzie seems to have this passage in mind when she writes of "the dangerous father who . . . could hurt the daughter if he wanted to." See *The Cure of Poetry in an Age of Prose: Moral Essays on the Poet's Calling* (Chicago: University of Chicago Press, 1993) 121. Leslie Heywood suggests yet another motivation: "the father 'never touches her' because according to cultural configuration she is different from him, feminine, and the speaker has seen this." See *Dedication to Hunger: The Anorexic Aesthetic in Modern Culture* (Berkeley: University of California Press, 1996) 43. Her reading finds some confirmation in the language of section 3, "Eros": "And the girl child / who wills herself / into her father's arms. . . ." Subsequent references to Heywood will appear in the text.

12. Upton, in a predominantly admiring discussion of Glück in *The Muse of Abandonment,* perceptively notes a kindred reservation: "In spite of her reiterations of the unwilled quality of mature poetry, the iconic character of Glück's prose and the vatic voice of her poetry are at odds with her argument. . . . The irony of her rejection of will is that Glück's prose and poetry generate much of their impact from what seems like the most strategic rhetoric. . . . For their impact, her poems rely on tone, and her own tone is one—for all her emphasis on the promise uncertainty holds—of extreme knowledge, even of fatedness. In fact, the omission of context in her poems raises multiple questions in the reader, and yet seldom allows for an impression that the speakers of her poems share in this bafflement about either cause or effect" (136). In "fatedness," cause and effect become monolithic, predestined; the historical particulars drop out because they can change nothing, since all must happen as it does.

13. See notes 8 and 21.

14. Susie Orbach, *Hunger Strike: The Anorectic's Struggle as a Metaphor for Our Age* (London: Faber and Faber, 1986) 24.

15. See Susan Bordo, "Anorexia Nervosa: Psychopathology as the Crystallization of Culture," in *Feminism and Foucault: Reflections on Resistance,* ed. Irene Diamond and Lee Quinby (Boston: Northeastern University Press) 94 (cited in Heywood, *Dedication to Hunger*).

16. See Lynn Keller, "'Free / of Blossom and Subterfuge': Louise Glück and the Language of Renunciation," in *World, Self, Poem: Essays on Contemporary Poetry from the "Jubilation of Poets,"* ed. Leonard M. Trawick (Kent: Kent State University Press, 1990) 129.

17. Sigmund Freud, *Beyond the Pleasure Principle* (1920), trans. James Strachey, rev. ed., (1961; repr., New York: Liveright, 1970) 30 (his emphasis). Subsequent references will appear in the text.

18. On the truth value of Freud's argument I remain agnostic, being unqualified to judge. I claim only that Glück imagines a death drive in terms strikingly akin to Freud's. I assume, since she mentions analysis explicitly in her poetry, that she is familiar with Freud's thought at least in broad outline.

19. Helen Vendler, *Soul Says: On Recent Poetry* (Cambridge: Harvard University Press, 1995) 16–17. "What the Flowers in the Meadow Tell Me" was Mahler's working title for the second movement of his Third Symphony. His flowers sound much happier than Glück's. Subsequent references to *Soul Says* will appear in the text.

20. Thanks to my wife, Jeanne Breslin, a gifted and experienced gardener, for a most helpful botanical consultation.

21. Binswanger describes Ellen West's pervasive sense of "the world as hole, tomb, or grave" (318). Again, Glück's is a kindred vision, though there are two crucial differences: she has climbed out and stayed alive, and she has evolved an original and powerful language in which to articulate her perceptions. Ellen West, on the evidence of the verse quoted in the case history and in Binswanger's own judgment, was a *poète manqué*.

22. Cf. Paul Celan, "Psalm": "Niemand knetet uns wieder aus Erde und Lehm, / niemand bespricht unser Staub. / Niemand. // Gelobt seist du, Niemand. / Dir zulieb wollen / wir blühn." ["No one moulds us again out of earth and clay, / no one conjures our dust. / No one. // Praised be your name, no one. / For your sake we / shall flower" (trans. Michael Hamburger).] Paul Celan, *Poems,* trans. and introd. Michael Hamburger (New York: Persea, 1980) 143.

23. Seamus Heaney, *The Government of the Tongue: Selected Prose 1978–1987* (New York: Farrar, Straus and Giroux, 1988) 17–18.

24. Seamus Heaney, *The Redress of Poetry* (New York: Farrar, Straus and Giroux, 1995) 153.

25. At the time this essay was written, *The Seven Ages* had not yet appeared.

SANDRA M. GILBERT

The Lamentations of the New

"I thought my life was over and my heart was broken. / Then I moved to Cambridge." Endings and beginnings, old lives and new starts: by a sort of Joycean vicus of (re)circulation, Louise Glück's *Vita Nova* ends with a casual, almost throwaway assertion of the premise that shapes its opening, for as if to emphasize the circularity implicit in the very idea of *re*newal, the book's final poem has the same title as its first lyric: "Vita Nova." And as if further to underline the urgency as well as the skepticism with which this poet approaches the very concept of newness, she inserts into her ambitious sequence a piece whose title translates the Latin *vita nova* into the English of "The New Life."

Vita Nova, not *Vita Nuova:* Glück's enterprise claims origins in Latin, not Italian; in classical Rome rather than thirteenth-century Florence; in the *Aeneid,* not the *Divina Commedia,* even while her substitution of a Latinate *nova* for Dante's *nuova* evokes the astronomical concept of a "variable star that suddenly increases in brightness," then fades or fizzles. To be sure, even in its revisionary feistiness, Glück's narrative of midlife endings and beginnings is haunted by Dante's equivocal record of the mingled lamentation and transfiguration associated with the loss of a beloved. But the radically different occasions that lead to loss dramatically underscore her subtle repudiation of the Florentine master: Dante simultaneously mourns and celebrates the death of an angelic lady, followed by her translation to the realm of the divine, while the author of (most recently) *Meadowlands* (1996) continues that book's often sardonic tale of a postmodern divorce and its outcome (*"my heart was broken. / Then I moved to Cambridge"*).

In addition, just as the metamorphosis of thirteenth-century mysticism into twentieth-century skepticism expresses the relationship between Dante's *Vita Nuova* and Glück's *Vita Nova,* a move from ecstasy to irony governs the structure of Glück's collection itself. Her first "Vita Nova"—the book's opening piece—is a mysterious meditation on the very process of beginning again. "You saved me, you should remember me," the poet tells an unnamed interlocutor, who may be a god, a muse, or even the life force that forms and informs both personal and impersonal regeneration:

> The spring of the year; young men buying tickets for the
>   ferryboats.
> Laughter, because the air is full of apple blossoms.
>
> When I woke up, I realized I was capable of the same
>   feeling.
>
> I remember sounds like that from my childhood,
> laughter for no cause, simply because the world is
>   beautiful,
> something like that.

Even here, however, the irony with which this poet examines the possibility of her own rebirth is implicit in her qualification of "simply because the world is beautiful"—her skeptical, distancing "something like that." Those who are wounded can heal (or *be* healed), this passage suggests, yet the very process of healing is inexplicable, even problematic, although it has its precedents in

> Crucial
> sounds or gestures like
> a track laid down before the larger themes
>
> and then unused, buried.

For Glück, in other words, as for T. S. Eliot—a twentieth-century poet even more frankly steeped in Dante—"April is the cruelest month" precisely because the rebirth of the "dead land" stirs memory as well as desire. Focusing on the "patches of new grass, the pale green / pieced into the dark existing ground," she excavates the roots of her own ambivalence. "Surely spring has been returned to me," she concludes with a mixture of exultation and sorrow,

>   this time
> not as a lover but a messenger of death, yet
> it is still spring, it is still meant tenderly.

By the time Glück rewrites her opening "Vita Nova" as the volume's concluding poem, once again a lyric entitled "Vita Nova," even the tenderest messages of death have been elided by the salutary toughness of a very funny (and plainly therapeutic) send-up of therapy and its discontents:

> In the splitting up dream
> we were fighting over who would keep
> the dog,
> Blizzard. You tell me
> what that name means.

Whatever Blizzard's name means, he evolves through a series of brilliant riffs into a poignantly comic avatar of the self in its effort at survival as the poet, in *her* effort at survival, recounts the dream, presumably for an unhelpfully clinical listener. I quote the remainder of the piece in its entirety:

> Poor Blizzard,
> why was he a dog? He barely touched
> the hummus in his dogfood dish.
> Then there was something else,
> a sound. Like
> gravel being moved. Or sand?
> The sands of time? Then it was
> Erica with her maracas,
> like the sands of time
> personified. Who will
> explain this to
> the dog? Blizzard,
> Daddy needs you; Daddy's heart is empty,
> not because he's leaving Mommy but because
> the kind of love he wants Mommy
> doesn't have, Mommy's
> too ironic—Mommy wouldn't do
> the rhumba in the driveway. Or
> is this wrong. Supposing
> I'm the dog, as in
> my child-self, unconsolable because
> completely pre-verbal? With
> anorexia! O Blizzard,
> be a brave dog—this is
> all material; you'll wake up

in a different world,
you will eat again, you will grow up into a poet!
Life is very weird, no matter how it ends,
very filled with dreams. Never
will I forget your face, your frantic human eyes
swollen with tears.
I thought my life was over and my heart was broken.
Then I moved to Cambridge.

Clearly the penultimate assertion—"Never / will I forget your face, your frantic human eyes / swollen with tears"—pertains at least as much to the speaker and her ex-beloved as to the bizarrely humanoid dog "Blizzard," with his curious if finicky taste for hummus and his soulful, tearful eyes in a canine skull. Thus Glück's "Never / will I forget" implies a farewell, followed by a hail: goodbye Blizzard and all you stand for; hello Cambridge, whatever *you* may mean. And of course the process through which the poet moves herself and her audience into this moment of *vale atque ave* is intricate and arduous. In one poem, whose English title—"The New Life"—still further emphasizes the various forms taken by the protest of the new against the old, the future against the past, she recounts the struggle for self-knowledge that must inevitably precede even the bitterest moments of regeneration:

I slept the sleep of the just,
later the sleep of the unborn
who come into the world
guilty of many crimes.
And what these crimes are
nobody knows at the beginning.
Only after many years does one know.
Only after long life is one prepared
to read the equation.

But in another piece, with the more utilitarian title "Nest," she endures and interprets yet another dream of the ways in which the nonhuman offers the human patterns for survival as well as for suffering.

Louise Glück's new poems have the weighty austerity of myth or, perhaps more accurately, the statuary of myth. At times, each sentence is pronounced as gravely as if it were spoken by lips of marble. Yet at other times, the poem's utterances—and often they are, indeed, portentous "utterances" rather than casual speech—seem torn from a small, far, suffering place that is beyond or behind the stony accretions of mythic sculpture. Glück's main concern as an artist has always been with the great questions myth and its statuary seek to ask (and answer): how to live, what to do. Principally, perhaps, how does the tiny being cope with its loneliness, how articulate and enact its burning frail desires? For around the posing and the resolution of such questions, after all, the weight of legend gathers. Ulysses chose *this* way, Penelope *that way,* yet Ulysses, Penelope, Aeneas, Eurydice, Dido, Orpheus—all, frozen in their tragic draperies—continue to wonder at their own choices. As Emily Dickinson once put it: "My husband—women say— / Stroking the melody— / Is *this* the way?"

JAMES LONGENBACH

Louise Glück's Nine Lives

Vita Nova, Louise Glück's eighth book of poems, begins with this enigmatic exchange between master and apprentice.

> The master said *You must write what you see.*
>
> But what I see does not move me.
>
> The master answered *Change what you see.*

Change is Louise Glück's highest value. Each of her books has begun, she admits, in a "conscious diagnostic act, a swearing off" of the work preceding it (*Proofs & Theories,* 17). But because of what Glück calls in *Vita Nova* her "inflexible Platonism," she is both entranced and threatened by "something beyond the archetype" ("Unwritten Law"). If change is what she most craves, it is also what she most resists, what is most difficult for her, most hard-won. And if her career has often moved forward at the expense of its own past, *Vita Nova* feels like the inauguration of a different kind of movement. Rather than retreating to an extreme of diction or sensibility, the poems of *Vita Nova* ultimately feel at home in a fluctuating middle ground that is not a compromise between extremes. Near the end of the book, the apprentice recognizes that she has internalized the lesson of the master:

> I have acquired in some
> measure
> the genius of the master, in whose supple mind
> time moves in two directions: backward
> from the act to the motive
> and forward to just resolution.
>
> —"The Mystery"

These lines characterize two narratives: one involves the place of *Vita Nova* in Glück's ongoing career, and the other is the story *Vita Nova* itself tells. To *write what you see* you must first *change what you see.* And if the past is the poet's subject, then the past must change: the inflexible Platonist must realize that the givens of experience are potentially as fluid, as mutable, as its possibilities. "I couldn't even / imagine the past," Glück admits at one point in *Vita Nova* ("Nest"). At another, when she asks herself if she feels free, all she can respond is that she recognizes the patterns of her experience. Throughout her career, Glück has often shown how the future runs on rails that are laid down not only in childhood but in lives preceding our own. But in *Vita Nova* the act of imagining the future is contingent upon the act of reimagining—rather than rejecting—the past. To change what she sees, the poet must write what she sees, changing what she sees in the process.

"The *Vita Nuova*," said T. S. Eliot, "is to my thinking a record of actual experience reshaped into a particular form."[1] Glück's title is brazen: she both courts Dante's specter and implicitly preempts it, titling her book with the Latin phrase that preceded Dante's vernacular. But like Dante's, her book is about the struggle to find what Glück calls "discernible form" ("The Mystery") for harrowing experience: the death of love and the rebirth of vocation. Glück has railed in her essays against narcissism in poetry; she has rejected the automatic prestige of forbidden subject matter. And by exploring the aftermath of a broken marriage in *Vita Nova*, Glück runs the risk—knowingly—of seeming merely sincere. But the real drama of *Vita Nova*, both thematic and structural, is the unfolding dialogue between "material" and "form," the way in which past experience is refigured in the language of poetry. "It must be done by speech," says Dante in Rossetti's translation, "or not at all."[2]

Glück's previous book, *Meadowlands*, was distinguished by its surprisingly wide discursive range—brash, vulgar, often funny. And while *Vita Nova* feels less austerely hieratic than much of Glück's earlier work, its poems by and large return to her more typically hushed idiom. But *Vita Nova* in no way signals a retreat. Glück's compulsion to change seems more substantive than ever before because *Vita Nova* does not represent a "swearing off" of the past: it accepts the notion that truly meaningful change must inevitably be partial change—complicit, incomplete. Speaking of her lifelong willingness to discard anything, Glück sees in herself the child she once was, a child "unwilling to speak if to speak meant to repeat myself" (*Proofs & Theories*, 18). In *Vita Nova*, Glück learns to live within repetition, and the result is, paradoxically, something really new: a reconsideration of the structure and function of lyric poetry.

Since the beginning of her career, the presiding technical problem of Glück's poems has been the placement of the speaker relative to the material. In *Firstborn,* her first book, the speakers seem involved in the emotional dilemma of the poems. But in the books that followed, Glück wrote a poetry distinguished more by its tone than by anything we could think of as a voice. Even the speakers of her dramatic monologues (often mythological figures) did not seem involved in the drama of their own lives. The novelist Michel Tournier has defined myth as "a story that everybody already knows," and it is in this sense that so many of Glück's poems seem mythic, whether their subjects are mythological or not. Her speakers know everything, and since everything has already happened, the poems feel spectral and eerily calm.

The poems also tend to culminate forcefully in their final lines. In 1975, Glück published a group of five poems, four of which would appear later that year in her second book, *The House on Marshland.* "Here Are My Black Clothes" sounds like a *Firstborn* poem; from the start, its speaker is agitated, its gestures dramatic: "I think now it is better to love no one / than to love you. Here are my black clothes." In contrast, "Messengers" is exquisitely placid but ultimately far more moving. Glück describes anyone's encounter with commonplace wild animals—geese, deer—but defers the significance of such encounters until the final lines:

> You have only to let it happen:
> that cry—*release, release*—like the moon
> wrenched out of earth and rising
> full in its circle of arrows
>
> until they come before you
> like dead things, saddled with flesh,
> and you above them, wounded and dominant.

In poems like these, Glück withholds the poem's attitude toward its material (rather than advertising it, as she does in the poems of *Firstborn*), and the result is an ending that directs our experience of the entire poem. "The love of form," Glück would say in *Ararat,* "is a love of endings" ("Celestial Music").

The uncanny power of poems like "Messengers" grows out of acts of willed renunciation: vigorous syntax, energetic rhythms, and colloquial diction had to be banished from this poetry. It is not surprising that from among the five poems published together in 1975, only "Jukebox" remains uncollected: "You hot, honey, do she bitch and crab, / her measly and depriving body holding back / your rights?"[3] As these lines suggest, Glück has always remained interested in the poetic possibilities she has renounced. But she was unable to find a place for this rough, colloquial diction in *The House on Marshland*, just as Yeats could not have worked the phrase "greasy till" into the symbolic world of *The Wind Among the Reeds* even if he'd wanted to.

The diction of *Ararat*, Glück's fifth book, is nowhere as energetic as in "Jukebox," but the poems do register Glück's will to change: throughout this sequence, written in the aftermath of her father's death, Glück forges a more intimate, less ghostly tone. But, as Glück has recognized of herself, she has "always been too at ease with extremes" (*Proofs & Theories,* 105), and it is telling that after the more colloquial *Ararat* she produced *The Wild Iris,* her most flagrantly symbolic book. It is her *Wind Among the Reeds*—a collection of disembodied lamentations and prayers: flowers address their gardener; the poet addresses God; and more profoundly, the poems address each other, creating a self-enclosed world of great poetic extravagance and—astonishingly enough—deep human feeling. But even when the poems adopt a point of view opposed to the poet's, the tone remains consistent:

> But John
> objects, he thinks
> if this were not a poem but
> an actual garden, then
> the red rose would be
> required to resemble
> nothing else, neither
> another flower nor
> the shadowy heart, at
> earth level pulsing
> half maroon, half crimson.
>
> —"Song"

These lines contain the seed of the dissatisfaction that would in turn produce *Meadowlands,* a book of different voices—some of them as rough as "Jukebox." Describing Yeats's development, Paul de Man once argued that *The Wind Among the Reeds* was a dead end because its words seem only to invoke other words, other associations, having relinquished their referential power.[4] Like the Yeats of *In the Seven Woods,* Glück struggles in *Meadowlands* to let the red rose "resemble / nothing else." She also recognizes that the refusal of resemblance inevitably depends on its perpetuation: only through metaphor ("the shadowy heart, at / earth level pulsing") may the rose be said to resemble nothing.

Throughout *Meadowlands,* the poet is challenged by the acerbic voice of her husband (who is also Odysseus): "You don't love the world," begins "Rainy Morning"; your "tame spiritual themes, / autumn, loss, darkness, etc.," are completely consistent with "the cat's pathetic / preference for hunting dead birds." In response, the poet (who is also Penelope) wants to entertain the possibility of including more of the world in her poems. But given the very nature of poetic language, the task is difficult. In "Parable of the Gift" Glück explains how she inadvertently killed a fuchsia plant by leaving it outside—by "mistaking it / for part of nature." The poem ends with a memory of a friend (who gave her the plant) bringing her "a towel of lettuce leaves":

> so much, so much to celebrate
> tonight, as though she were saying
> here is the world, that should be
> enough to make you happy.

These lines epitomize the dilemma of *Meadowlands.* Glück is tired of reading the world as if it were an emblematic tapestry, yet she finds it difficult to be sustained by natural things alone. What's more, she has trouble distinguishing the natural from the emblematic. "As part of nature he is part of us," said Stevens of the poet, but it's not easy for a poet who mistakes a plant for "part of nature" to take this wisdom for granted.

In "Nostos" (perhaps the most beautiful poem in the book) Glück remembers an apple tree that seemed, year after year, to flower on her birthday: seen once, it immediately became an emblem for consciousness, as did every subsequent apple tree she encountered:

> Substitution
> of the immutable
> for the shifting, the evolving.
> Substitution of the image

for relentless earth. What
do I know of this place,
the role of the tree for decades
taken by a bonsai, voices
rising from the tennis courts—
Fields. Smell of the tall grass, new cut.
As one expects of a lyric poet.
We look at the world once, in childhood.
The rest is memory.

Like "Messengers," "Nostos" culminates scrupulously in its final
lines; it is the kind of poem Glück has mastered. But the poem's de-
lineation of a timeless lyric space is balanced throughout *Meadowlands* by a desire for disruptive forward motion—"that pulse which
is the narrative / sea." However representative of Glück's achievement, "Nostos" must be read in dialogue with the rougher poems of
Meadowlands. The voice exhorting Glück to abandon "tame spiritual
themes" in "Rainy Morning" is really her own: she wants sincerely
to push at the boundaries of what "one expects of a lyric poet."

Even if any word she uses is fraught with emblematic significance
and can never be "natural," the multiple voices of *Meadowlands* allow
Glück to harness words and rhythms that could never have sat comfortably even in *Ararat.* She is also free to be funny: the brash or
deadpan poems, especially those spoken by the weirdly prescient son
(who doubles as Telemachus), sound especially humorous when juxtaposed with poems like "Nostos." Still, this very strength—the
achievement of a wholeness of feeling greater than its parts—may
have relieved Glück from the pressure to transform herself more
substantively. No matter how many times Glück writes a poem like
"Rainy Morning," poems like "Nostos" or "Parable of the Gift"
nonetheless stand comfortably beside poems like "Messengers."

If *Meadowlands* first seemed like a sign that Glück was expanding
her range, the appearance of *Vita Nova* now makes *Meadowlands* feel
ominously like a dead end. It offered Glück two mutually exclusive
choices: she could continue to write hushed, luminous poems like
"Nostos," or she could write brash, acerbic poems like "Rainy
Morning." But how much more skeptical, more disillusioned—
more pick-your-adjective—could the author of lines like "your cold
feet all over my dick" ("Anniversary") become? Glück's scrupulous
talent for self-interrogation is capable of generating its own illusions.
"Romance is what I most struggle to be free of," she has said (*Proofs*

& *Theories,* 8), but there is a romance bound up in the need never to be deceived, the need always to see through ourselves before somebody else gets a chance. It is a romance of purity, a romance that leads us to be more comfortable in extremes than in the middle. More difficult than heaven or hell, says Glück apropos of Eurydice, is the act of "moving between two worlds" ("Eurydice"). *Vita Nova* is her book of the difficult middle.

Like *Meadowlands, Vita Nova* demands to be absorbed in one long reading. But *Vita Nova* is built around not one but two mythic backbones—the stories both of Dido and Aeneas and of Orpheus and Eurydice: the book's structure consequently feels like an intersection of various narratives rather than the unfolding of a single one. In addition, Glück's position relative to these narratives is fluid. At one moment the poet will align herself with Dido or Eurydice, but at the next, her condemnation of Orpheus's narcissism will seem directed as much at herself as at the lover who has abandoned her: "Tell them there is no music like this / without real grief" ("Orfeo"). Because Glück recognizes her complicity, the poems don't feel neatly opposed to each other even when they take on opposing personae. If *Meadowlands* exteriorizes as dialogue the conflicts lyric poems more often interiorize as ambiguity, *Vita Nova* is uttered by a single speaker who contains within herself a variety of overlapping, eccentric positions.

This strategy is appropriate to the book's subject since, as I began by suggesting, the poems of *Vita Nova* concern not so much the breakup of a marriage as the poet's subsequent attempt to reorder her experience—to provide "discernible form" for "available material." On the one hand, the poet is cut off from the future; the marriage she thought was eternal has succumbed to time. On the other hand, she is cut off from the past; she remembers how her mother turned away "in great anger" because she had "failed to show gratitude" for her mother's love: "And I made no sign of understanding. // For which I was never forgiven" ("Timor Mortis"). This "never" is the dead center of *Vita Nova:* it signifies a past that is beyond our control but which continues to control us, delimiting our experience in the present.

Throughout most of the first half of *Vita Nova,* Glück despairs of the possibility of meaningful change. As in "Nostos," she feels that we enter the world "guilty of many crimes," that the soul is as a result "inflexible." Paradoxically, it is the end of the marriage—the source of despair—that offers an antidote to despair. In "Unwritten Law" the poet seems weirdly grateful to the husband who abandons her: if she gave herself to him "absolutely," he, in his "wisdom and cruelty," taught her "the meaninglessness of that term." He taught her, so to speak, that the word "never" is only as shifting and deceptive as the word "forever," that the material of our experience is never beyond change.

Our job is not to "recognize [the past] 'the way it really was,'" said Walter Benjamin, but to "seize hold of a memory as it flashes up at a moment of danger."[5] Glück's passionate commitment to change is born of a fear of irrefutable memory—of the possibility that, as in "Nostos," we are permitted to look at the world only once. Throughout the second half of *Vita Nova,* she consequently begins to fight back, seizing hold of the past when it threatens to determine her future. In "Nest" she describes a dream in which she watched a bird construct its nest from the "available material" left in the yard after other birds have finished their weaving:

> Early spring, late desolation.
> The bird circled the bare yard making
> efforts to survive
> on what remained to it.
>
> It had its task:
> to imagine the future.

The bird's task is of course Glück's. In dreams as in poems she moves—like the master who instructs her—in two directions at once: by moving forward into the future she also moves backward into the past, altering it, commanding it. In "Condo" her dream even confuses past and future, "mistaking / one for the other."

There is nothing merely innocent or inevitable about the confusion: "*Bedtime,*" whisper the leaves in "Evening Prayers," "*Time to begin lying.*" But however desperate Glück feels in the face of intractable material, her "struggle for form" does move toward moments of repose. "Formaggio" begins with lines that sound like the end of a typical Glück poem:

> The world
> was whole because
> it shattered. When it shattered,
> then we knew what it was.

The triumph of "Formaggio" is that it moves beyond what feels like an ending, reconstructing a world. After the world shattered, says Glück, human beings built smaller worlds in the fissures: "blocks of stores" (Fishmonger, Formaggio, Hallie's flowers) are like "visions of safety"; "salespeople" are "like parents," only "kinder than parents." In this "provisional" world the recognition that Glück has "had many lives" is for once liberating. She is even willing to repeat the phrase:

> I had lives before this, stems
> of a spray of flowers: they became
> one thing, held by a ribbon at the center, a ribbon
> visible under the hand. Above the hand,
> the branching future, stems
> ending in flowers. And the gripped fist—
> that would be the self in the present.

These final lines of "Formaggio" are liberating both because of what they say (emphasizing the way in which a self is constructed over time rather than predetermined) and because of the way they follow on the previous lines of the poem. The poem sets a scene— a block of stores on Huron Avenue—and weaves a meditation in and out of the scene, implicitly paralleling the poet's casual movement from store to store: the poem's final image of the self gripping its previous lives feels like the wonderfully unpredictable result of having ended a day's journey in Hallie's flower shop. "The place you begin doesn't determine / the place you end," says Glück in "Nest." Coming from the author of "Nostos," this realization is the source of all freedom in *Vita Nova*.

For the simple reason that they repeat language that has already occurred earlier in the poem, the final lines of "Formaggio" feel spontaneous rather than weighty, part of an ongoing process rather than grandly conclusive. Repetition: while Glück laments in "Unwritten Law" that "the mistakes of my youth / made me hopeless, because they repeated themselves," she eventually recognizes in "The Garment" that "when hope was returned to me / it was another hope entirely." To exist in time is necessarily to exist in repetition; to exist successfully in time is to recognize that what is returned to us—hope or despair—repeats the past with a difference. Once we recognize that difference, then the past is changed; it becomes a source of possibility. But however powerful in itself, this realization wouldn't matter much if Glück presented it in poems that, like "Messengers" or "Nostos," carry their weight in their final lines. The real achievement of *Vita Nova* is a new kind of lyric structure, one that embodies a love of the middle rather than a "love of endings."

In the first poem called "Vita Nova" Glück revisits the scene of "Nostos"—the apple tree that determines her experience of all subsequent trees. This time, Glück looks at the scene again and again. Her meditation stutters, returning to the scene of the apple tree with fresh observations. She compares the memory to a scene in the present; she wonders if she's remembered correctly. "Crucial / sounds or gestures" from childhood may be "laid down" like a track, but rather than feeling doomed to repeat them, Glück feels enabled by repetition—"hungry for life." In the poem's final lines, spring repeats itself but with a difference:

> Surely spring has been returned to me, this time
> not as a lover but a messenger of death, yet
> it is still spring, it is still meant tenderly.

The difference is the recognition of mortality—the recognition that we live in time. If "Nostos" offers what "one expects of a lyric poet"—a timeless lyric space—"Vita Nova" offers a new sensibility in a new structure. Like "Formaggio," "Vita Nova" exists more firmly in the repetitive turnings and hesitations of its middle than in its conclusion; it embodies the movement of a story without telling one.

None of these more dialogically structured poems employs the rougher diction that characterizes many of the poems of *Meadowlands*. Only the second poem called "Vita Nova" recalls the idiom of *Meadowlands,* and it is telling that this poem concludes with highly charged final lines. It seems to me that after testing her signature idiom in *Ararat,* honing it in *The Wild Iris,* and exploding it in *Meadowlands,* Glück realized that the changes were in danger of seeming cosmetic: her poetic structures—and the determinism they embodied—remained unchallenged. Ellen Bryant Voigt has recently written about how, at least since the New Criticism, we have tended to focus on form, diction, and tone, leaving poetic structure (which is not necessary coequal with form) to take care of itself.[6] Poems like "Formaggio," the first "Vita Nova," "Aubade," "Castile," "Ellsworth Avenue," and "Lament" do not flagrantly expand Glück's idiom but offer instead a more meaningful change, a change that reaches through a poem's skin to its bones.

These poems seem more intricately dialogical than the poems in *Meadowlands* or *Vita Nova* that are structured as actual dialogues. Since they don't split into different voices, their movement feels endless and manifold rather than end-stopped and oppositional. Because the poems repeat and revise themselves, the dialogue takes place within their very linguistic texture. Even if the same thing could be said of the texture of an earlier poem such as "Mock Orange"—

> It is not the moon, I tell you.
> It is these flowers
> . . . .
> I hate them.
> I hate them as I hate sex

—these repetitions feel static, intentionally wooden, and the poem feels liberated from repetition when its syntax finally arcs across the line:

> In my mind tonight
> I hear the question and pursuing answer
> fused in one sound
> that mounts and mounts and then
> is split into the old selves,
> the tired antagonisms.

In contrast, the dialogical poems in *Vita Nova* seek no liberation from repetition—neither formally nor thematically. (And it is telling that they feature longer lines and less enjambment than most of Glück's earlier poems.) Since Glück has abandoned her staunch determinism, freedom may now be found within the unfolding of the poem rather than at its conclusion. Speaking of Robert Pinsky's "At Pleasure Bay" (a poem structured through the repetition of the phrase "never the same"), Glück has noted that the implication of the phrase changes subtly with each repetition and consequently "stands for recurrence even as it asserts the absence of perfect duplication." She could be speaking here of "Formaggio" or of the first "Vita Nova." The poem "finds in shift and movement what lyric [traditionally] uses stopped time to manifest," Glück continues;

through its "relentless mobility," it offers "an unfolding, a pattern, as opposed to . . . iconic stasis."[7]

In her own "Castile" Glück does not repeat a single phrase but a group of phrases that recombine throughout the poem in different ways: "orange blossoms," "children begging for coins," "I met my love," "the sound of a train," "I dreamed this." The poem begins by setting a scene:

> Orange blossoms blowing over Castile
> children begging for coins
>
> I met my love under an orange tree

But Glück immediately questions this memory, wondering if the orange tree might have been an acacia tree, speculating that the memory might have been a dream. The poem seems to start over several times, moving in and out of the scene, simultaneously presenting it and questioning it:

> Castile: nuns walking in pairs through the dark garden.
> Outside the walls of the Holy Angels
> children begging for coins
>
> When I woke I was crying,
> has that no reality?
>
> I met my love under an orange tree:
> I have forgotten
> only the facts, not the inference—
> there were children somewhere, crying, begging for coins

Because each repetition of a phrase occurs in a slightly altered context, the phrases feel both different and the same. And their movement consequently embodies the fluid, errant sense of memory that the poem describes. Near the end of "Castile" the speaker remembers that she gave herself to her lover "completely and for all time"—or so she thought: the poem's final image of movement confirms the vicissitudes both of love and of poetry:

> And the train returned us
> first to Madrid
> then to the Basque country

If the poems Glück has written since *Firstborn* feel like records of events that have already happened—myths—the dialogical poems like "Castile" feel like events that are happening. They stand among the most intricate and beautiful poems Glück has made.

Glück's embracing of repetition seems to me the crucial development in *Vita Nova:* the structure of the poems, their attitude toward change, and their relationship to Glück's earlier work all depend on it. Having seen repetition as Platonic recollection, in which everything new looks backward to its original source, Glück now understands repetition as Walter Benjamin described it in his magisterial essay on Proust: "Is not the involuntary recollection, Proust's *mémoire involuntaire,* much closer to forgetting than what is usually called memory?" While our "purposive remembering" dissipates "the ornaments of forgetting," Proustian memory looks forward rather than holding us hostage to an unchanging past: it discovers future possibilities by recognizing that what repeats is always subtly different from itself.[8]

"A terrible thing is happening—my love / is dying again," begins "Lament," the penultimate poem in *Vita Nova.* "How cruel the earth," says Glück, "the willows shimmering." Then again: "My love is dying." But surely: "Once is enough." Yet again: "The willows shimmer by the stone fountain." And again: "Once is enough." And again:

> My love is dying; parting has started again.
> And through the veils of the willows
> sunlight rising and glowing,
> not the light we knew.
> And the birds singing again, even the mourning dove.
>
> Ah, I have sung this song. By the stone fountain
> the willows are singing again.

"Ah, I have sung this song": this sigh of recognition is the crowning moment of *Vita Nova.* Throughout "Lament," Glück mourns not the loss of her lover but the loss of her mourning: what will Orpheus have to sing about? The acceptance of repetition (which is the acceptance of mortality) allows memory to become a kind of forgetting; it allows her to imagine a future beyond the death of the death of love. It also enables her to live in the present, in the middle of life, rather than seeking shelter in extremes of language or sensibility. In "Earthly Love" (which stands beside "Immortal Love") Glück describes a couple who were held together by the "conventions of the time," conventions requiring them "to forfeit liberty" without their knowing it. The end of the marriage was in this sense fortunate, since it dissipated the romance of convention. "And yet," says Glück—

> And yet, within this deception,
> true happiness occurred.
> So that I believe I would
> repeat these errors exactly.

These are mighty lines for a poet who has said that she disdains the illusions of romance above all else, a poet who has said that she would rather keep silent than repeat herself. The lines themselves repeat the work of another reformed Platonist, the Yeats of "A Dialogue of Self and Soul"—

> I am content to live it all again
> And yet again

—the Yeats who was astonished at the bitterness of *The Tower* and subsequently embraced the fury and mire of experience in *The Winding Stair*. Yeats is, famously, a poet whose every new volume offers a new Yeats. "It is myself that I remake," he counseled readers early on.[9] But Yeats is also a poet whose every line is identifiable as his alone. *Vita Nova* sounds more like the Louise Glück we know than *Meadowlands,* but given the real innovation in poems like "Castile" and "Lament," that familiarity is the book's power. Having recognized that real freedom exists within repetition rather than in the postulation of some timeless place beyond it, Glück now seems content to work within the terms of her art—resisting them from within rather than turning against them. The result is a book suggesting that Glück's poetry has many more lives to live.

NOTES

1. T. S. Eliot, *The Varieties of Metaphysical Poetry,* ed. Ronald Schuchard (New York: Harcourt, 1993) 97.

2. *La Vita Nuova,* in *The Portable Dante,* trans. D. G. Rossetti, ed. Paolo Milano (New York: Penguin, 1975) 601.

3. Louise Gluck, "Jukebox," *Antaeus* 17 (spring 1975): 67.

4. See Paul de Man, *The Rhetoric of Romanticism* (New York: Columbia University Press, 1984) 162–72.

5. Walter Benjamin, *Illuminations,* ed. Hannah Arendt (New York: Schocken, 1977) 255.

6. See Ellen Bryant Voigt, "The Flexible Lyric," in *The Flexible Lyric* (Athens: University of Georgia Press, 1999) 114–71.

7. Louise Glück, "Story Tellers," *American Poetry Review* 26 (July–August 1997): 12.

8. Benjamin, *Illuminations,* 122.

9. W. B. Yeats, *The Variorum Edition of the Poems,* eds. Peter Allt and Russell K. Alspach (New York: Macmillan, 1957) 778.

JOANNE FEIT DIEHL

"From One World to Another"
Voice in Vita Nova

If the poems of *Vita Nova* bear a resemblance to forms we have
encountered earlier in Glück's work—the mythic persona; the
dream narrative; the ironizing dialogue; the stark, lyric cry—
these materials are put in the service of a newly modulated voice
that turns to the world with an openness, an eagerness to embrace
experience that is far from the estranged sensibility that haunts
earlier poems. By "eagerness," I do not mean a sloughing off of
the burden of self-consciousness to render contact between self
and world innocent; instead, this new turn to the world is the turn
of the survivor, of one who has passed through crisis and found
fresh, imaginative territory for the continuation of her art. *Vita
Nova* is, simultaneously, the record of the poet's journey to this
discovery and a rendering of how her poetry alters in the light of
this discovery.

   Both the opening and closing poems of this volume are entitled
"Vita Nova," and each announces a distinct kind of beginning.
The first poem's opening line, "You saved me, you should remember me," with its compelling appeal to a power or individual bearing redemptive gifts, will be repeated in "Seizure," a poem late in
the book that witnesses another kind of transformation. In the first
"Vita Nova" a dream of youths laughing in spring leads the
speaker to the realization that she "was capable of the same feeling." Memories from childhood add to this aura of pleasure, and
another dream, this time of her mother "holding out a plate of
little cakes," leaves her when she awakens "elated, at my age / hungry for life, utterly confident." And yet the exuberance of these
dreams and associations confronts a haunting terminus; when
spring returns, it is "not as a lover but a messenger of death." Yet
the confident voice at poem's close testifies to both a recognition
of the presence of death and an acceptance of the hope spring carries with it:

> Surely spring has been returned to me, this time
> not as a lover but a messenger of death, yet
> it is still spring, it is still meant tenderly.

This openness to the benign possibilities of the world marks a turn from the more austere aesthetics of abstinence that characterize much of Glück's earlier work.

Similarly, the volume's next poem, "Aubade," signals an awakening to the pleasures of the material world: to color, texture, and change. Before dawn, the world inside the brain is colorless, "all / interior space," inviolate but to the ravages of time. So different is the current consciousness's experience that this earlier dread of time is itself barely remembered: "I took time very seriously in those years, / if I remember accurately." The grief at the center of that former self leads to two conflicting desires: "desire / to be safe and desire to feel." The choice for feeling is experienced not as coming from within, but from without as, with growing light, objects are slowly delineated, colors glow. And time, too, becomes infused with the desire to be malleable, to be alive to change: "somewhere // time stirring, time / crying to be touched, to be / palpable." The recognition of the material world, like the awakening from dream in "Vita Nova," returns the speaker to her childhood:

> and then I was once more
> a child in the presence of riches
> and I didn't know what the riches were made of.

The mysterious plenitude reexperienced by mature consciousness awaits exploration; and part of this volume's poetic project is to present a growing acquaintance with that plenitude. But it is only a part, for the poems that follow attest as well to a desire to render extreme affective states and to attend to Glück's familiar dramas of suffering, which inform an only partial turn from grief.

As in Glück's earlier volumes, most especially *The Triumph of Achilles* and *Meadowlands,* several poems in *Vita Nova* speak through mythic or epic presences. The voices of Dido, Francesca, and Eurydice—the abandoned, the punished, and the betrayed—resonate with the consequences of passion. "The Queen of Carthage," "The Burning Heart," "Eurydice," and "Relic" speak to life beyond the end as they reflect upon the vicissitudes of love; poems of aftermath, they look back upon the outcome of longing. But each poem accomplishes more as it imagines the unique conditions that inform this love, giving voice to the powerful exigencies that arise as a woman contemplates her fate. In "The Queen of Carthage," Dido calls upon her ladies-in-waiting "that they might see / the harsh destiny inscribed for her by the Fates." In the aftermath of Aeneas's desertion, Dido asserts that she "will accept suffering as she accepted favor"; she makes of destiny a willed and conscious choice. What further dignifies her action is her closing reinterpretation of fate itself:

> Now the Queen of Carthage
> will accept suffering as she accepted favor:
> to be noticed by the Fates
> is some distinction after all.

> Or should one say, to have honored hunger,
> since the Fates go by that name also.

The Fates are here identified with the force of one's own desire, the inescapable yearning that Dido honors in her pursuit of the fulfillment of her passion for Aeneas. Dido's expression of this desire as hunger is significant, for it is one of a number of instances in this volume where hunger, instinctual physical need, is not only acknowledged but valorized. The recognition that hunger enacts one's destiny is a major theme here as in Glück's earlier books, a hunger that represents the force of fate.

"Eurydice" chooses to focus on a similar moment, when Eurydice's lover has been lost, converting what could be conceived as passive acquiescence to loss of the world into a choice against what the poem interprets as Orpheus's faithlessness:

> Only for a moment
> when the dark of the underworld
> settled around her again
> (gentle, respectful),
> only for a moment could
> an image of earth's beauty
> reach her again, beauty
> for which she grieved.

> But to live with human faithlessness
> is another matter.

The tug of earth's beauty cannot vie with the closing lines' understated judgment. The patent unacceptability of living with "human faithlessness" is given as the reason that informs Eurydice's acceptance of her return to the underworld, a revision of the myth which affords her moral agency and self-determination. The understated tone in which Eurydice's decision is expressed only intensifies its authority. In both "The Queen of Carthage" and "Eurydice," Glück seizes upon moments in the narratives when fate traditionally speaks. By restoring language and thereby the power of choice to Dido and Eurydice, these poems expand the expressive possibilities of writing as a survivor and thereby asserting agency over experience.

It is to these expressive possibilities that Glück turns when she evokes Orpheus in "Lute Song" and "Orfeo"—not only to the musical powers of Orpheus but to the human consequences of such gifts. The object of universal desire, Orpheus is "made present / not as a human being, rather / as pure soul rendered / detached, immortal, / through deflected narcissism." That deflected narcissism, which robs Orpheus of human attributes, mistakes the nature of his all-too-human quest; for his lute, originally made to "perpetuate the beauty of [his] last love," has become "the struggle for form" and his dreams "less the wish to be remembered / than the wish to survive," a wish he believes to be "the deepest human wish." The elegiac impulse gives way before the more fundamental desire for survival as the reality of human instincts de-idealizes the hitherto narcissistically conceived and imaginatively projected image that is Orpheus. "Orfeo," a companion poem to "Lute Song," opens with a traditional lament, only to shift abruptly to a voice conscious of the operative possibilities of its own performance as the speaker relishes the quality of his own voice and the beauty of the songs he sings. Later, the singer recognizes the general distrust of the preoccupations of the artist, as if these somehow rendered him less human in others' eyes. Orfeo's hesitancy regarding others' perceptions of his artistic powers causes him to question the divine origins of his gift:

> And who knows, perhaps the gods never spoke to me in
>   Dis,
> never singled me out,
> perhaps it was all illusion.

Orfeo addresses Eurydice with resentment: having married him for his art, what right has she to want "human comfort?" Chafing under the burden of her demand, he distrusts what she might tell the furies if they should meet. Therefore, he endows Eurydice with his own message:

> Tell them I have lost my beloved;
> I am completely alone now.
> Tell them there is no music like this
> without real grief.

The poem closes with Orpheus expressing his assurance that the furies will recall his voice: "In Dis, I sang to them; they will remember me." Wishing to be known only through the beauty of his voice, Orfeo separates his resentment and distrust of Eurydice from the romantic legend he has come to believe. Ironically, the illusion of his unambivalent devotion to his beloved and his consequent desolation when they are parted inspire his music, the myth of unalloyed love and isolation fueling Orfeo's belief that his music's origin lies in "real grief." Could authentic feeling be released by belief in an illusion? Such is Orfeo's self-authenticating conviction.

A more ruminative and introspective sensibility belongs to Glück's Aeneas, whose early resentment at being born belatedly, after the accomplishments of Greek civilization, gives way to "faint contempt for the Greeks, / for their austerity, the eerie / balance of even the great tragedies— / thrilling at first, then / faintly predictable, routine" ("Roman Study"). With this shift in attitude comes an awareness of what remains for Aeneas uniquely to accomplish as he recognizes with fortuity how exactly suited he is to the descriptive task at hand:

> And the longer he thought
> the more plain to him how much
> still remained to be experienced,
> and written down, a material world heretofore
> hardly dignified.
>
> And he recognized in exactly this reasoning
> the scope and trajectory of his own
> watchful nature.

The project suits his nature because it is born of it; attentiveness to a "material world heretofore / hardly dignified" becomes Aeneas's new life. Through his distinctive cast of learning, a process that

yields "a new species of thought entirely, / more worldly, more ambitious / and politic," Aeneas discovers the nature of his aesthetic
bent, the "scope and trajectory of his own / watchful nature." This
predilection of the watcher, an attentiveness to the material world,
reminds us of a more general aspect of the Glückian poet's avowed
project—a renewed receptivity to the world's materiality.

In a poem that recounts the poet's rediscovery of her materials
in relation to the story of a bird's "making its nest," in a "poem of
the mind in the act of finding / What will suffice" (Wallace
Stevens, "Of Modern Poetry"), Glück reveals the nature of the
bird's quest and its necessity: "It took what there was: / the available material. Spirit / wasn't enough" ("Nest"). For the speaker observing the work of the bird, its ritual of preparations, however, no
such action is possible. The bird "had its task: / to imagine the future," but the speaker "had nothing to build with. / It was winter:
I couldn't imagine / anything but the past. I couldn't even / imagine the past, if it came to that." The bird's deliberate activity stands
in stark contrast to the speaker's helplessness. Yet, with a suddenness
placed wholly outside the self, a change in season provokes an inexplicable change of mood, a centering:

> Then it was spring and I was inexplicably happy.
> I knew where I was: on Broadway with my bag of groceries.
> Spring fruit in the stores: first
> cherries at Formaggio. Forsythia
> beginning.

As her mood shifts from resignation to "flashes of joy," the speaker's
attention moves outward:

> And as I peered out my mind grew sharper.
> And I remember accurately
> the sequence of my responses,
> my eyes fixing on each thing
> from the shelter of the hidden self:

> first, *I love it.*
> Then, *I can use it.*

Emotion precedes the will to activity as the love the speaker invests
in the material leads to a recognition of the possibilities for its use.

This turn to experience and recognition of its usefulness is the subject of "Descent to the Valley," which maps not a shift in seasons but the span of a life. Contrary to the speaker's theoretical expectations of "the shape of a human life: / on the one side, always upward and forward / into the light; on the other side, / downward into the mists of uncertainty," experience has revealed it "otherwise." Freed now from the anxieties of the ascent, the speaker finds a sweetness that had formerly eluded her. And with this vision of the valley as "fertile and tranquil" comes the will toward experience that inhabits the closing lines of "Descent to the Valley":

> How sweet my life now
> in its descent to the valley,
> the valley itself not mist-covered
> but fertile and tranquil.
> So that for the first time I find myself
> able to look ahead, able to look at the world,
> even to move toward it.

This impulse toward the world is new in Glück's poetry, which has more often registered the rigors of a stoical resistance.

Yet this new openness, this embrace of the material world, is but one side of an aesthetic dichotomy; for in *Vita Nova,* Glück's impatience with the obdurate world and its stubborn resilience to the imposition of human form survives. This impulse of opposition is compellingly articulated in "The Winged Horse," wherein the speaker summons her Platonic horse, "Abstraction," to take her far beyond the world of material limitation. "Abstraction's" wild freedoms compel the speaker, who is "weary of [her] other mount, / by Instinct out of Reality," "weary of being opposed," "and weary of being constantly contradicted by the / material, as by / a massive wall where all I say can be / checked up on." The will toward immortality fuels the speaker's desire as she makes her appeal: "Come, Abstraction, / by Will out of Demonic Ambition: / carry me lightly into the regions of the immortal." Patient receptivity to the world of the incremental is rejected out of hand, and in its place is the impatience of a mind pleading to be carried "where you have taken so many others, / far from here, to the void, the star pasture." The closing, terse command, all swiftness—"Bear me quickly, / Dream out of Blind Hope"—nevertheless raises a new complexity: Does the speaker's dream of "Abstraction's" power arise from a hope that is blind, desperate in its refusal of sight, or does this dream carry the speaker away from the blindness of hope into the fulfillment of creative ambition? Surely, these alternatives centering around the ambiguities of "out of" raise antithetical possibilities for interpretation. If the speaker's yearning for abstraction stems from blind hope, it is futile or, at best, unguided; if, on the other hand, her yearning escapes such hope to recover an alternative relation to experience, she may break through to a greater expressive freedom. The speaker asks that "Abstraction" "bear her quickly," as if she must make her escape before it is too late. The urgency of the imperative is countered, however, by the uncertainty relating to the origins of the speaker's desire, by the ambiguities associated with the equivocal phrase, "Dream out of Blind Hope."

This complication of motive, introduced so fleetingly in "The Winged Horse," is further addressed in a series of question-and-answer poems, in which straightforward, objective-sounding questions are responded to with oblique, sometimes Delphic replies. Modeled upon Dantean dialogue, "The Burning Heart," "Timor Mortis," "Mutable Earth," and "Inferno" reveal inflections of the psychoanalytic voice of objectivity attempting to prompt the analysand's memory. Taking for its epigraph lines from Robert Pinsky's translation of *The Inferno*—"No sadness / is greater than in misery to rehearse / memories of joy"—"The Burning Heart" loosely recalls the story of Paolo and Francesca, but without the circumstantial specificities that would delimit the poem's occasion. Mediating his or her questions through an interlocutor (as, of course, Dante uses Virgil), the first speaker asks a series of questions, repeating him- or herself as if the question has not been directly addressed. This form allows for an interesting kind of freedom; for, while the structure of the interlocutory serves to shape the narrative response, that response nevertheless is free to reassign emphases and define meaning to construct its own story. A tension arises caused by the gap between sought-for response and what is actually produced, and this strain contributes its own emotional valence to the narrative, as what is withheld or revised becomes as crucial as what is revealed. Thus, the dialogue of question and response creates a texture of subtle inflections as the answers inform the questions by what they will and will not disclose:

> Ask her if the fire hurts.

> I remember
> we were together.

And gradually I understood
that though neither of us ever moved
we were not together but profoundly separate.

Ask her if the fire hurts.

You expect to live forever with your husband
in fire more durable than the world.
I suppose this wish was granted,
where we are now being both
fire and eternity.

Do you regret your life?

Even before I was touched, I belonged to you;
you had only to look at me.

Frustrated by the apparent evasion of his or her questions, the interlocutor fails to notice that another story is being told, a story of awakening to the realization of the lovers' reality in hell. The second time
the question, "Ask her if the fire hurts," receives an answer; a reply
that suggests an ironizing acceptance of their fate. And the response to the final question, "*Do you regret your life?*" is directed not
to the interlocutor but to the woman's lover, a performative gesture
that in itself speaks to the commitment as well as intensity of her love.

Questions of a different kind are asked in "Timor Mortis," where
present fear is linked to childhood memories. Here the quasi-
analytic promptings of the interlocutor stir up dream associations
and self-revelation. Again the dialogue functions through indirec-
tion as repeated questions elicit images, reflections, and insight. Indeed, these questions function as a kind of insistent refrain that fo-
cuses on the issues to be addressed. With such incursions into
memory come understanding and self-interpretation which culminate in the recounting of a rejection with lasting consequences as
the speaker's mother turns away from her impassive daughter:

And I remember once my mother turning away from me
in great anger. Or perhaps it was grief.
Because for all she had given me,
for all her love, I failed to show gratitude.
And I made no sign of understanding.

For which I was never forgiven.

The psychological impasse is, for Glück, a familiar one; what is interesting poetically is the rhetorical process that has produced this occasion, the call-and-response structure that complicates self-revelation through mediation. By the time we win through to an understanding of the origins of the second speaker's fear of death, we have already been introduced to a pattern of disclosure which is interrelational instead of unitary, to a process of inquiry which emerges from two voices instead of one. This duality alters the fundamental character of self-disclosure, substituting for the declamatory a more nuanced, interactive cadence.

The effect of the reiterated, climactic question in "Mutable Earth," another poem that employs the question-and-answer frame, is somewhat different from that of "Timor Mortis." Here the insistent questioner appears to extract from the respondent a more refined and clarified expression through the sheer necessity of yet again answering the same question:

> But do you think you're free?
>
> I think I recognize the patterns of my nature.
>
> But do you think you're free?
>
> I had nothing
> and I was still changed.
> Like a costume, my numbness
> was taken away. Then
> hunger was added.

The speaker bears witness to a change that appears neither self-willed nor self-controlled. Instead, the poem traces the struggle between the speaker's "vigilance," resisting any change because it would feel like loss, and the uncontrollable forces of life that affect transformation. Like the change in mood that occurs with the change of season in "Nest," a change that precipitates a life's revolution, the changes evoked here are carried out, or at least are perceived as being carried out, for a force beyond the self. Hunger, which elsewhere stands in for desire, a turn outward toward the world, here is imposed by what is experienced as external force. This perception of being acted upon and the acceptance of change enacted by something or someone beyond the self are a part of the relinquishment of control vital to the new energies of *Vita Nova;* the psychic position of anorexia has given way to a less defended, more assured awareness of the permeable self.

The complexities of consciousness increase in "Inferno," wherein question and response lead to the recognition that the experiential self has undergone a change that she can only partially fathom. Memories of a fire twenty years ago merge with recollection of a dream in which she builds a funeral pyre for herself. The answer to the question, "Why did you move away?" is at first answered by the respondent's own amazed questioning: "I walked out of the fire alive; / how can that be?" The dreamer outlasts her yearning for self-destruction, her belief that she "had suffered enough":

> I thought this was the end of my body: fire
> seemed the right end for hunger;
> they were the same thing.

Whereas in "Mutable Earth" hunger is represented as an apparently energizing and appetitive quality, here hunger seeks to be consumed. And yet, when the self awakens from her dream to discover that fire has not destroyed her, when she enters a different world of whose character she cannot be certain, the speaker experiences "not the end of need but need / raised to the highest power." By choosing "Inferno" as the poem's title, Glück underscores the possibility that the speaker inhabits a fiery afterlife, has left one fire for another. Whatever the "truth" of the situation, the self experiences a change of world of the most compelling sort. The irony of that change resides in the new world's not obliterating but rather heightening need; whatever world the self now inhabits creates the conditions that promote difference, and with that difference, a new field of action upon which "need / raised to the highest power" determines the course.

In addition to this mode of dialogic interaction, Glück draws on other forms from her repertoire to witness her altered relation to reality. Turning to the biographical and the anecdotal in "The Mystery," she relates her mastery of a Nero Wolfe novel (wherein she has learned the principles of motive and retribution) to the utterly arbitrary nature of her life. Written from the viewpoint of aftermath, the poem acknowledges:

My life took me many places,
many of them very dark.
It took me without my volition,
pushing me from behind,
from one world to another.

. . . .

And it was all entirely arbitrary,
Without discernible form.

The passionate threats and questions,
the old search for justice,
must have been entirely deluded.

Yet this arbitrariness does not detract from the "amazing things" she witnesses, things that transformed her life so that she "became almost radiant at the end." But just because life will not reveal its motives does not negate the self's yearning for answers, the continued sense of injustice which provokes renewed accusations. To resist her own accusations, the speaker turns to her book:

I carried my book everywhere,
like an eager student
clinging to these simple mysteries

so that I might silence in myself
the last accusations:

Who are you and what is your purpose?

Articulating her accusations in the act of silencing them, Glück is attracted to the prophylactic nature of a fiction predicated on a belief in cause and effect and notions of objective justice to enforce her punitive demand that the as yet inchoate forces that drive her life identify themselves and declare their intent.

Elsewhere, as in "Evening Prayers," the speaker imagines a hoped-for solace whose source is compassion: "I construct a presence / wholly skeptical and wholly tender, / thus incapable of surprise." Yet this will to belief is matched by the speaker's deep distrust of her own motives, a distrust murmured by the leaves of a little birch tree:

I can feel
the leaves stir, sometimes
with words, sometimes without,

as though the highest form of pity
could be irony.

Bedtime, they whisper.
Time to begin lying.

Yet the speaker believes that her prayer, uttered before the birches'
whispering, has itself been a lie: "the request for help / masking request for favor / and the plea for pity / thinly veiling complaint."
The words spoken by the tree acknowledge its acceptance of this
untruth and further whisper that bedtime, the quotidian ritual that
recalls death itself, may, alternatively, be the time for lying. The
ironizing pun affirms Glück's characteristic yoking of the deceptive
and the ordinary. In her "unhappiness," the speaker imagines a listener who is endowed with her own skepticism but whose presence is also "wholly tender," a presence that accepts the inevitability of such deception, while proffering compassion.

This fusing of skepticism and tenderness marks a turning point
in *Vita Nova,* and the volume's final poem, in its mediating of these
qualities through the valence of humor, articulates the accomplishment implicit in its form. The apparent subject of the final "Vita
Nova" is immediately identified by category: a presentation and interpretation of "the splitting up dream." The telling of the dream is
punctuated with questions addressed sometimes to the speaker's
former partner and sometimes to herself. With dream logic, the
narrative presents a series of scenes: the couple "fighting over who
would keep / the dog, / Blizzard," Blizzard barely touching "the
hummus in his dogfood dish," "a sound" and associations on the
sound: "The sands of time?" "Then it was / Erica with her mara-
cas." These disjunct images give way to the ruse of finding a language in which Blizzard can understand the family breakup. Speaking in the pared-down language reserved for young children and
pets enables Glück simultaneously to preserve irony while invoking a form of comic regret:

> Blizzard,
> Daddy needs you; Daddy's heart is empty,
> not because he's leaving Mommy but because
> the kind of love he wants Mommy
> doesn't have, Mommy's
> too ironic—Mommy wouldn't do
> the rhumba in the driveway.

The narrative voice effortlessly draws parallels between Blizzard and the speaker's own "child-self," "unconsolable because / completely pre-verbal? With / anorexia!" What follows constitutes the deflected offering of consolation to that child-self. Enjoining Blizzard to be a "brave" dog, the speaker assures him that "this is / all material." Suffering can be put to use; transformation is possible. Consolation resides in the comically absurd prophesy that Blizzard will be transformed from pet to poet:

> you'll wake up
> in a different world,
> you will eat again, you will grow up into a poet!

Acknowledging that "Life is very weird, no matter how it ends, / very filled with dreams," the speaker reminds Blizzard, her child-self, and us of what the poems in this volume so frequently reveal: the seeming randomness, the apparently aleatory nature of experience, and the concomitant proliferation of fantasy. Keeping faith with the child-self's suffering, "your frantic human eyes / swollen with tears," the speaker maintains contact with that early pain. Without apparent transition, the poem swiftly and brilliantly concludes:

> *I thought my life was over and my heart was broken.*
> *Then I moved to Cambridge.*

The very transformation that the speaker has promised Blizzard is here enacted; change has occurred, change from grief to a new life. The crafty, deflationary shift in tone from the high romantic locution, "my heart was broken," to a "plaine-style" recounting of fact serves as a form of shadow play that simultaneously registers the equivocating sorrows of the inner life and the consolations of external geography. This swift tonal shift signifies the more encompassing conceptual project of Glück, for, while tapping the roots of suffering, it nevertheless embraces the possibility of a transformative freedom. The maturity that informs this hard-won affirmation is the mark of a poet at the height of her powers. If the poems of *Vita Nova* testify to Glück's verbal mastery of her materials, as they assuredly do, so, in their ironic tenderness, they locate their source in a renewed engagement with the world. Glück's imagination, open to chance and to fate, informs the voice of *Vita Nova,* a voice at once skeptical, passionate, new.

STEPHEN YENSER

Louise Glück's New Life

Some years ago I placed a telephone call to Plainfield Village, in Vermont, where, in an unnumbered house on what I imagined to be an idyllic Creamery Road (I had a return address on an envelope to work with), Louise Glück was living, at least when she was not out of town, as she increasingly was those days, reading her poems, or being a visiting poet at some university, or teaching at Warren Wilson College in Swananoa, North Carolina, where she had been a founding and famously devoted member of the MFA program in creative writing (which program she had helped birth at Goddard College–but that's another story). I had never spoken with her, and I was calling to confirm arrangements having to do with her upcoming trip to UCLA. To my mild disappointment, the call did not have to go through "Central." She herself picked up the phone right away and was to the point about absolutely everything, so all too quickly our conversation was . . . over. Plainfield indeed. Partly Quaker by heritage, I knew austerity when I encountered it—whether even or especially in a woman whom I knew to be Jewish I couldn't say—and I resisted. In a last, hopeless moment I asked how the *weather* was in central Vermont. On the other end of the line there was a pause—wary and palpable, or in Wallace Stevens's phrase (as I thought the next day) of "a sudden concentration as of cloudy weather." And then a single throaty word, distantly threatening: "Imminent." Her address notwithstanding, the new "milkmaid poet" she was not.

And that was that. But my extension of the phone call and our choice for that quarter's featured reader were instantly justified. "*Imminent* weather." It was the sort of adjective that, like the new companion of an old friend you've really become too accustomed to, makes you look at the friend with new eyes. ("Ya know, there's somethin' to be said for ol' Belle Wether after all.") It was a superb adjective, at once unexpected and unimprovable. What else could a certain weather be but "imminent"—which is of course to say, etymologically, "overhanging." I could have been listening to Eve between her encounters with the serpent and with Adam. "Imminent." It seemed to me that Emily Dickinson might have been inspired to vivify the Latinism in just that way. (I later checked the concordance. Dickinson used the adjective four times but never with a comparable literalness. Indeed, I can find no explicit indication that Glück has read Dickinson closely, a possibility that I find arresting since no one else of her approximate age reminds me as often of Dickinson as the earlier Glück. Lucie Brock-Broido and Alice Fulton have recently and eloquently recorded their different debts to Dickinson, but their sensibilities ostensibly have less in common than Glück's with hers.)

In its utter accuracy, the accuracy of its utterance, her pointed response was characteristic—not just of her telephonic manner, to be sure, but of her poems as well. And when shortly thereafter I learned that her last name was not pronounced like the famous composer's but rather to rhyme with "click," and that her father had held the original patent on the Exacto knife, I could hardly credit the switchblade-quick connections. At that point, she had published three volumes of poems—*Firstborn, The House on Marshland,* and *Descending Figure,* and a fourth—*The Triumph of Achilles*—was in the works. Each volume was, I suppose, minimal in length, at least by publishers' expedient standards; the poems in each rarely ran more than a page, except when they were sequences of short poems; and the lines, which always worked away from an iambic norm, often had but two or three stresses. Taut, compressed, they reminded me of "the hard, active buds of the dogwood" she said she had seen one day on a walk. And the poems were indeed themselves "hard"—again, rather in the way that Dickinson's can be hard. Not inscrutable, but charged. Potent. Maybe sexual. Robert Frost's pronouncement that he disliked "obscurity" but adored "dark statements" sprang to mind. Dickinson, thinking of her own lyrics, surmised that "Could mortal lip divine / The undeveloped Freight / Of a delivered syllable / 'Twould crumble with the weight." She would have known that "undeveloped" means "not unwrapped" or "not unrolled," whereas its mate "delivered" means "freed," so her comparison might be paraphrased thus: *liberated like a baby from the womb but with a future still wrapped up as though in swaddling clothes.* Glück too had an acute sense of the syllable's tremendous freight, and so she was brief.

Because she demanded of herself both precision and succinctness, her poems entailed considerable linguistic torsion. They made you wonder what in another era her telegrams might have been like—and what she might have accomplished in that most constraining of contemporary forms, the so-called vanity license plate (she turned out not to drive). Her poems often invented paradoxes, set puns with delayed fuses, and contrived other means of compassing complexity economically. So she would touch on "the terrible charity of marriage," and would see that in a certain situation a reflecting mind would be "stricken with light," and would remind us how "the past, as always, stretched before us." Such phrases controlled even as they formulated a special intensity. They had—her poems had—something of the "passionate . . . restraint" she had observed in a scene at the Palais des Arts, and her work reminded me of Yeats's desideratum: a poetry "cold and passionate as the dawn." It reminded me also of Yeats's assertion that "patient pains and passionate impulse are not incompatible." (He made his point in part by invoking three words—"patient," "passionate," and "compatible"—that come from the same Latin source, meaning "to suffer.")

Then somehow, before I knew it, Louise Glück, who had established herself as a writer of extravagant economy—a poet so terse and dense that the careful reader could hardly turn a leaf with one hand—had published eight volumes. Hers was a body of work not only weighty in particular parts but also ample as a whole—as the judges for the esteemed Bobbitt Prize (now *there's* a suitable name for a prize given to a minimalist poet at the end of the twentieth century), and the judges for the Pulitzer Prize, as well as those for the National Book Critics Circle Award and the William Carlos Williams Award, kept confirming. Having woven this chaplet of honors together, she published a collection of writings on poetry entitled (with exemplary brachylogy) *Proofs & Theories.* Spare, Spartan, if not downright taciturn, it includes a plangent three-page essay on "Death and Absence," a six-page paean to "Impoverishment," and a twelve-page meditation—a veritable tome in this context—called "Disruption, Hesitation, Silence." A great admirer of George Oppen, she tells us in one of these essays that his art is "bold, severe, mysterious, intense, serene, and fiercely economical." With the notable exception of "serene," these fastidious if uncharacteristically numerous adjectives are strikingly applicable to much of her own work.

Economy is not necessarily a virtue that inspires approbation. I am not able to think, for instance, of a single Greek or Roman figure, apart from Penelope (whom Glück invokes for altogether different purposes in *Meadowlands*), who glorifies economy. The Fates are not necessarily frugal, and Procrustes clearly will not do. While we have goddesses of plenty aplenty, the deities of parsimony are scarce indeed. Which is doubtless just as it should be. Still, starting with the proverbial "Silence is golden"—a proposition that tarnishes itself in its very utterance—there is a good deal to be said for saying comparatively little. (To those interested in the ultimate subject, I recommend P. L. Heath's dazzling and hilarious entry on "Nothing" in *The Encyclopedia of Philosophy,* which demonstrates vividly how much has been said of that matter—or of the absence of matter altogether.) We all recognize the truth in Mies Van der Rohe's aphorism, "Less is more," just as we all applaud the wisdom of Coco Chanel's advice, "Take off the last thing that you put on." John Cage made compositions out of the texture of "silence"; certain prized Japanese ink drawings, like Zen gardens, are positively full of emptiness; the abstract impressionists doted on negative space; and for his part Matisse maintained that the scissors he used to make his late cutouts executed a more sensitive line than the pencil. Her goal too, the earlier Glück implies, is to be at once absent and present—or to be more specific, laconic and eloquent, chary and rich, astringent and energetic.

Her seventh volume, *Vita Nova,* as far as its poetics goes, sometimes seems equally committed to a certain austerity and minimalism. We find there a number of paradoxical maxims, reminiscent of the earlier poems, ingenious, wiry, and gratifying as pipe-cleaner creations:

> Just because
> the past is longer than the future
> doesn't mean there is no future.
> —"Condo"

> I slept the sleep of the just,
> later the sleep of the unborn
> who came into the world
> guilty of many crimes.
> And what these crimes are
> nobody knows at the beginning.
> Only after many years does one know.
> —"The New Life"

> I think sometimes
> our consolations are the costliest thing.
> —"Relic"

                    Destruction
          is the result of action.
                                    —"Inferno"

              It was a period
              (very long) in which
              the heart once given freely
              was required, as a formal gesture,
              to forfeit liberty: . . .
                                    —"Earthly Love"

          I was afraid of love, of being taken away.
          Everyone afraid of love is afraid of death.
                                    —"Timor Mortis"

     And here too are the minor, faintly metallic ironies, some almost
invisible and all the more effective for that. Many years ago, Glück
wrote a nearly perfect little lyric called "For Jane Meyers" which is
as savagely fresh now as it ever was. These are the last stanzas of a
poem that might actually withstand a comparison with George
Herbert's "Vertue" (which masterpiece, in just four fewer lines,
epitomizes a spring "full of sweet dayes and roses, / A Box, where
sweets compacted ly / . . . And all must dy"):

          Look how the bluet falls apart, mud
          pockets the seed.
          Months, years, then the dull blade of the wind.
          It is spring! We are going to die!

          And now April raises up her plaque of flowers
          and the heart
          expands to admit its adversary.

The opening poem in Glück's seventh volume—entitled, like the
last poem, "Vita Nova"—comes to rest with this version of that
earlier thought that April is the cruelest month:

          Surely spring has been returned to me, this time
          not as a lover but a messenger of death, yet
          it is still spring, it is still meant tenderly.

Two views—or at least two tones—fade into each other here as smoothly as the enjambed lines override the syntactical units, and the balance struck is tipped word by word in the last line in the direction of melancholic irony. It is not "still spring," of course, the repetition of that first word notwithstanding, precisely because spring by nature cannot be "still" (whether as adjective or adverb) but inevitably comes and goes and in its going becomes "a messenger of death." And in Glück's atheistic world, spring is not "meant" by anyone to suggest anything, so the term "tenderly" is garnish provided by the poet, who is perhaps all too aware that it is a decorative adverb.

At the same time, however, *Vita Nova* (not exactly Dante's title, we note—and indeed, for better or worse, Glück connects the new life with the *loss* rather than the discovery of a beloved) purports to be the beginning of a new mode—or at least the end of the old one. Further, the book often indicts the poet's own earlier manner, as in "Unwritten Law," a poem early in the collection in which erotics and aesthetics (as so often) overlap:

> Interesting how we fall in love:
> in my case, absolutely. Absolutely, and, alas, often—
> so it was in my youth.
> And always with rather boyish men—
> unformed, sullen, or shyly kicking the dead leaves:
> in the manner of Balanchine.
> Nor did I see them as versions of the same thing.
> I, with my inflexible Platonism,
> my fierce seeing of only one thing at a time:
> I ruled against the indefinite article.

But that earlier "Platonism" or absolutism, however much regretted, proved hard to shed. Here is the second half—precisely the second half—of the same poem:

> And yet, the mistakes of my youth
> made me hopeless, because they repeated themselves,
> as is commonly true.
> But in you I felt something beyond the archetype—
> a true expansiveness, a buoyance and love of the earth
> utterly alien to my nature. To my credit,
> I blessed my good fortune in you.

Blessed it absolutely, in the manner of those years.
And you in your wisdom and cruelty
gradually taught me the meaninglessness of that term.

So the poem repeats itself as the "mistakes" have done, and
then repeats the alleged correction of the compulsiveness ("But
in you . . . "), even as it reasserts by way of a bitter pun on "buoy-
ance" the earlier fascination with boyishness, and then iterates the
original sin ("Blessed it absolutely"), before finally apparently renouncing altogether the notion of the absolute. But the logic of
the poem and its momentum suggest an endless cycle—and suggest it strongly enough that the reader cannot but hear the incip-
ient pun in Glück's terminal word. The "meaninglessness" of any
"term" is the meaninglessness of an *end* or *limit,* and the poem,
though almost in spite of itself, implies not a renunciation of absolutism but rather an addiction to an oscillation between ardent
absolutism and weary skepticism. As she phrases a related quandary at the end of "Earthly Love," where the illusion of a conse-
crated union is the subject:

> And yet, within this deception,
> true happiness occurred.
> So that I believe I would
> repeat these errors exactly.
> Nor does it seem to me
> crucial to know
> whether or not such happiness
> is built on illusion:
> it has its own reality.
> And in either case, it will end.

The same conflict twists "Descent to the Valley" into its peculiar
shape. This poem recalls without adornment or false modesty the
poet's steep "climb upward" earlier in her career and her attendant
belief that the proper direction was perfectly clear if nonetheless
demanding:

> on the one side, always upward and forward
> into the light; on the other side,
> downward into the mists of uncertainty.
> All eagerness undermined by knowledge.

But she was wrong, she now thinks, partly because the (absolute) "light of the pinnacle . . . the goal of the climb, / proves to have been poignantly abstract" and partly because the (skeptical)

> mind, in its ascent,
> was entirely given over to detail, never
> perception of form; my eyes
> nervously attending to footing.

While clearly not written by an entirely new woman ("footing" has a fussy prosodic dimension, to take one instance), these lines epitomize a powerful critique of Glück's earlier work. She had always been preoccupied with "form," hitherto often a tyrannical adversary. "The soul's like all matter: / why would it stay intact, stay faithful to its one form, / when it could be free?" she asks in *Ararat* ("Lullaby"). But "form" emerges in *Vita Nova* as a *generating* concept, a concept of an organization that, instead of consisting before the fact to corral its particulars, clears the way for them. Given this broader view—this view *as it were* from the pinnacle, her paradoxical repudiation of the summit notwithstanding—the lower geographical reaches, which correspond to the poet's current location, are the preferred region:

> How sweet my life now
> in its descent to the valley,
> the valley itself not mist-covered
> but fertile and tranquil.
> So that for the first time I find myself
> able to look ahead, able to look at the world,
> even to move toward it.

Glück's echo of the Twenty-third Psalm, though faint, is unmistakable. The question that the passage therefore poses is as follows: is her assertion about the sweetness of the new life in "the world" and the implicitly liberating view of "form" to be taken at face value? Or is that assertion a whistling in the dark? In other, mundane terms: can we believe her? Or does her claim that she can "move" forward amount to a repetition of the alleged earlier error, the location of original and ultimate Meaning in a single position or recognition? If we were to answer that last question in the affirmative—that is, if we were to suppose that the new life equals sweetness, fertility, and form as newly perceived—the next question would be: is Glück's claim knowing and ironic and thus slyly erosive of the conclusion that the poet's life is now "sweet"—or are her lines to be understood earnestly to proclaim a true beginning rather à la Matthew Arnold? In either case, what are the ramifications for the quality of her poems?

I have no confidence that such questions can be answered except—and then sometimes ambiguously—in the cases of particular poems. The issue is further complicated by my apprehension that the poems in *Vita Nova* deflect and defer criticism of them individually. That is, I understand *Vita Nova* as a cohesive project, a constellation if not a sequence, that springs from opposing forces or impulses, which Glück names or alludes to repeatedly. At the risk of occluding these poems' nuances and tangles, and with the proviso that I want soon to mitigate the dichotomies, I set down what I take to be some fundamental contraries and allied conditions in *Vita Nova:*

The Old Life	*The New Life*
Fear	Desire
Smallness	Amplitude
Place	Places
Soul or mind	Body
The individual body	Bodies
Protection	Touch
Containment	Release
Self-deception	Clarity
Fences and walls	The universal "star pasture"
Opposition, limitation	Freedom, liberty
Greeks	Romans
Riparian tributaries	Ocean
Ascent	Descent
The heavens	Earth
Hades	Earth
Eurydice	Orpheus

One thing that's missing, of course, is a word for the *interaction* of the two factions or impulses—the knot that they tie, untie, retie. I have to think that, until a better term presents itself, the previewed "form" itself will have to suffice. As far as I can tell, "form" in the *Vita Nova* poems is the product of the *agon* between the two forces somewhat factitiously arrayed above. To put that in a different way, when Glück writes in a poem in *Ararat* that "The love of form is a love of endings" ("Celestial Music"), her pronouncement now seems Delphic: to love form (or worship death) is, alas, to obviate beginnings; and to love endings (or worship life) is to facilitate beginnings. *Vita Nova,* while acknowledging the former truth, stresses the latter, and her new book *The Seven Ages* moves further in the direction of reconciliation with the world of change.

An artfully constructed book, like all of Glück's volumes, *The Seven Ages* begins with its title poem, which in a move characteristic of this collection revisits both the early work and the early world of the poet: "In my first dream the world appeared / the salt, the bitter, the forbidden, the sweet. . . . In my first dream the world appeared / the sweet, the forbidden / but there was no garden only / raw elements." "The Seven Ages" acknowledges a succeeding phase:

> In my second I descended
>
> I was human, I couldn't just see a thing
> beast that I am
>
> I had to touch, to contain it
> . . . .
> I had to beg to descend
> the salt, the bitter, the demanding, the preemptive
>
> And like everyone, I took, I was taken
> I dreamed
>
> I was betrayed:
>
> Earth was given to me in a dream
> In a dream I possessed it

The title *The Seven Ages* does not refer as much to Jaques's set piece in *As You Like It* as to the ogygian tradition that one's life goes through recognizable stages, anywhere (according to the ancients) from three to nine. (The Louise Nevelson wood sculpture reproduced flip and flop on Glück's handsome dust jacket evokes both a cello and the female figure and features seven circular forms.) In Glück's volume one detects signs of a phase that follows on the writer's attainment of the age of fifty, a milestone she refers to several times, and in which phase increasingly we find something akin to contentment or satisfaction.

Consider these excerpts:

I had drawn my chair to the hotel window, to watch the rain.

I was in a kind of dream or trance—
in love, and yet
I wanted nothing.

—"Eros"

that the only constant
was distance, the servant of need.
Which was used to sustain
whatever fire burned in each of us.

The eyes, the hands—less crucial
than we believed. In the end
distance was sufficient, by itself.

—"The Ruse"

I lay awake, listening.
Fifty years ago, in my childhood.
And of course now.
What was it, speaking to me? Terror
of death, terror of gradual loss;
fear of sickness in its bridal whites—

When I was seven, I believed I would die:
only the dates were wrong. I heard
a dark prediction
rising in my own body.

I gave you your chance.
I listened to you, I believed in you.
I will not let you have me again.

—"Saint Joan"

I take it that the "you" there is "Terror," who is implicitly dismissed also in the embrasures in "Summer Night":

Desire, loneliness, wind in the flowering almond—
surely these are the great, the inexhaustible subjects
to which my predecessors apprenticed themselves.
I hear them echo in my own heart, disguised as convention.

Balm of the summer night, balm of the ordinary,
imperial joy and sorrow of human existence,
the dreamed as well as the lived—
what could be dearer than this, the closeness of death?

I do not mean that Glück has completely mellowed. Even now, as
she puts it in "Youth," she always hears "Sad sounds of our growing up— / twilight of cellos. No trace / of a flute, a piccolo." Reeds
would suggest a lighter, even comedic spirit—at the beginning of
the war of instruments, when it was winds vs. strings, Marsyas took
everything more lightly than Apollo, with results that were of
course appalling—and Glück has rarely shown us a sense of humor.
(I remember that when I talked to her after the reading mentioned
at the beginning of this ramble, her poem "Aphrodite," which she
had read, came up because I praised it. She thanked me and said
that she had enjoyed writing it, partly because it was the funniest
thing she had written, so that she had been surprised to hear from
a fellow poet that he had thought it so touchingly sad. I was glad
not to have to take sides.)

The question of her affinity for levity apart, the recent poems
testify to a sense of acceptance hitherto rare in Glück's work. When
the irremediably curmudgeonly William Logan characterizes *The
Seven Ages* as the product of a woman who "has whipped her
poems into tedious resentment," "luxuriating angst," and an "ecstasy of grief," he overlooks, willfully or no, precisely Glück's critique and modification of her own trajectory before *Vita Nova*. In
that previous life, Glück admits in "Birthday," she was "suffused /
with contempt for the communal, the ordinary," "consigned to
solitude," and "completely dominated by the tragic" and the illusion that her "ideas" were "the truth." She confesses that she ig-
nored "the world":

Meaning the partial, the shifting, the mutable—
all that the absolute excludes. I sat in the dark, in the living room.
The birthday was over. I was thinking, naturally, about time.
I remember how, in almost the same instant,
my heart would leap up exultant and collapse
in desolate anguish. The leaping up—the half I didn't count—
that was happiness; that is what the word meant.

If the reference to Wordsworth's notorious lines is surprising, it nonetheless illuminates by conjuring a starkly different sensibility to measure Glück's old one by. The allusion might serve a further purpose: the Wordsworth who believed in 1802 that "The Child is father of the Man" also wanted his exultation at the sight of a rainbow never to change. Glück (whose name in German of course means "happiness," as she wants us to remember when we read that last line) now discovers felicity when she acknowledges change. Has the erstwhile classicist caught the father of the volatile Romantics with his Absolute up?

In any event, the poet who by her most recent account once admired "the attempts of the mind / to prevent change" ("Birthday") and who "didn't want / the leaves turning, the nights turning dark early" ("Radium") now treasures the metamorphic world, "evolving or malleable," that "begins / to shift and eddy around us, only now / when it no longer exists" ("Youth"). Now it is not the static, abstract, other realm that the poems seek but rather "the physical world" or "the earth, / the same / disappearing sweetness," which she epitomizes in "Ripe Peach." She puts the point succinctly: "Fifty years. Such a long walk / from the door to the table." The "door" once opened on an escape, on the "separate joys" of "the mind" which she compared to "the night sky" with its "fiercest stars" or "immaculate distinctions." The "table," on the other hand, invites acceptance and participation. One almost hears the speaker in Herbert's "Love (3)": "So I did sit and eat." Perhaps more to the point is Yeats's Self, who disdains Soul's summons to the "breathless starlit air" and chooses instead the "blind man's ditch," with its own fecundity, fatality, and withal its "sweetness."

In poems like "Ripe Peach" and "The Sensual World," with its "stewed plums, stewed apricots," and various juices, Glück's images remind us somewhat of the later Yeats and his appetites. Far more often, however, her language has a closer relationship with one of Yeats's younger contemporaries. These are the opening lines of her "Reunion":

> It is discovered, after twenty years, they like each other,
> despite enormous differences (one a psychiatrist, one a city
>   official),
> differences that could have been, that were, predicted:
> differences in tastes, in inclinations, and, now, in wealth

(the one literary, the one entirely practical and yet
deliciously wry; the two wives cordial and mutually
    curious).
And this discovery is, also, discovery of the self, of new
    capacities:
they are, in this conversation, like the great sages,
the philosophers they used to read (never together), men
of worldly accomplishment and wisdom, speaking
with all the charm and ebullience and eager openness for
    which
youth is so unjustly famous. And to these have been added
a broad tolerance and generosity, a movement away from
    any contempt or wariness.

In the seemingly lackadaisical yet confident gait of the meditation,
the fondness for balance and repetition, parallelism and conjunctive
beginnings, and the abstract diction, this excerpt has to be modeled
on the discursive sections of Eliot's *Four Quartets*. And here in "The
Traveler" is what is surely Glück's version of the "dead master"
episode in "Little Gidding," where the poet and interlocutor is addressed by a "stranger" who is also a "familiar compound ghost." In
Glück's emblem the speaker is standing beneath a tree on which
the fruit has rotted:

And after many years, a traveler passed by me
where I stood, and greeted me warmly,
as one would greet a brother. And I asked why,
why was I so familiar to him,
having never seen him?

And he said, "Because I am like you,
therefore I recognize you. I treated all experience
as a spiritual or intellectual trial
in which to exhibit or prove my superiority
to my predecessors. I chose
to live in hypothesis; longing sustained me.

In fact, what I needed most was longing, which you seem
to have achieved in stasis,
but which I have found in change, in departure."

The dangers in conjuring such a "dead master" or rival "predecessor" as Eliot will be as evident as the inescapable differences between

the two poets. For one thing, whereas Eliot was delicately echoing
Yeats, Shakespeare, Dante, and others, including his own Stetson, and
in the course of doing so offending the early readers of the *Quartets*
with an utterly original blend, Glück is imitating Eliot. For another
thing, whereas Eliot was measuring out a firm long line, Glück
writes a loose free verse that here depends chiefly on breath-group
lineation and elsewhere (especially when her line is shorter, as it
more characteristically is) relies in contrast on heavy enjambment.
Moreover, a closer analysis could show how much finer Eliot's gra-
dations of diction are than Glück's. In a parenthesis near the end of
"Little Gidding," where he commends a text in which

> every word is at home
> Taking its place to support the others,
> The word neither diffident nor ostentatious,
> An easy commerce of the old and the new,
> The common word exact without vulgarity,
> The formal word precise but not pedantic,
> The complete consort dancing together[,]

Eliot embodies that text as well. He has assayed to a gram such
words as "commerce," "common," "vulgarity," and "consort," in addition to "word" itself, which is such a fulcrum in his sequence.
When he wants to increase the dynamics we get passages like the
one in the "dead master" episode where he criticizes his earlier
work and assumptions: "These things have served their purpose: let
them be. / So with your own, and pray they be forgiven / By others, as I pray you to forgive / Both bad and good. Last season's fruit
is eaten / And the fullfed beast shall kick the empty pail."

Another difference has to do with tone. There is sometimes in
Eliot, as there is in the later Yeats before him, an enthusiasm, a *jouissance,* that Glück can only allude to, as when she hesitantly approaches the subject in "Grace":

> The miraculous, the sublime, the undeserved;
> the relief merely of waking once more in the morning—
> only now, with old age nearly beginning,
> do we dare to speak of such things, or confess, with gusto,
> even to the smallest joys.

The "smallest joys" include "Affection, dinner with friends, / And
the structure of certain / adult tasks" and thus strikingly recall

Eliot's "moments . . . of well-being, / Fruition, fulfillment, security or affection, / Or even a very good dinner" in "The Dry Salvages." But his contrasting "moments of happiness," or *Erhebung,*" do not have a parallel in Glück, whose "smallest joys" include also

> The day unfurling, but very gradually, a solitude
> not to be feared, the changes
> faint, barely perceived—
> the penstemon open.
> The likelihood
> of seeing it through to the end.

If the "it" of her last line refers to the "day," the tone is wry; if "it" refers to the life, the tone is bitterly ironic. Glück's inflections are mostly in the range established by these two tones.

The exultant moment in *The Seven Ages* occurs near the end of "Mitosis" in a vision, or a "dream" of the future that is dreamed by "the body":

> Limitless world! The vistas clear, the clouds risen.
> The water azure, the sea plants bending and sighing
> among the coral reefs, the sullen mermaids
> all suddenly angels, or like angels. And music
> rising over the open sea—

The "mermaids" of "The Love Song of J. Alfred Prufrock," a poem that has meant much to her (as she shows in an essay in *Proofs & Theories*), become angelic, and their music is no longer private and exclusive but welcoming—for a moment. But in the end, the body's dream is not radically different from "the dream of the mind," which used to prevail in that relationship, although the body's dream is more satisfyingly melancholy, apparently because the poet now realizes that body and mind were never divided:

> The same sea, the same shimmering fields.
> The plate of fruit, the identical
> violin (in the past and the future) but
> softer now, finally
> sufficiently sad.

It is not necessarily my point that contentment makes for stronger poems than sadness, although Eliot himself seems to have thought so, and Dante's epic is after all the *Commedia*. In "The Protean Encounter" Howard Nemerov has addressed the issue in terms that might echo *Four Quartets,* which of course echoes St. Julian of Norwich: "The greatest poetry sees clearly and says plainly the wickedness and terror and beauty of the world, while at the same time humming to itself, so that we overhear rather than hear: All will be well." One can see, nay, hear Glück's sneer of a smile.

But my point is that, against her own steely resistance, the originally anxious, absolutist, minimalist Louise Glück has opened her poems up. In her beginning, she thinks now, Perfection was her God and *le mot juste* was the hammer in God's sculpting hand: "Night and day, I revised my appeals, // making each sentence better and clearer, as though one might / elude forever all misconstruction. How flawless they became— / impeccable, beautiful"—but, she sees, "continuously misread" ("Ancient Text"). In those days "The world was a detail, a small thing not yet / exactly right. . . . / What was real was the idea" of the world which she could herself institute ("August"). Those days were extensions of her youthful summers, when she went with her family to the beach: "I sat with my legs arranged to resemble / what I saw in my head, what I believed was my true self. // Because it *was* true: when I didn't move I was perfect." The result, she implies, was an art that didn't move; the hard buds of the dogwood rarely flowered. Be that as it may, the poems in the last two volumes move—and, to my mind, they are therefore the more moving.

To admit the imperfect nature of the idea of the flawless is not, of course, to take a step toward perfection. *The Seven Ages* is an eminently mortal volume. As I have suggested earlier, its meters are often slack, and its language is sometimes so relentlessly abstract in one way or another that it cannot avoid cliché:

> Waves of despair, waves of hopeless longing and heartache.
> Waves of the mysterious mild hungers of youth, the dreams
>   of childhood.
>
> —"Fable"

> After a time, I realized I was living
> a completely idiotic life.
> Idiotic, wasted—
> and sometime later, you and I

began to correspond, inventing
an entirely new form.

> —"From a Journal"

I'm alone—all
My riches surround me.
I have a bed, a room.
I have a bed, a vase
Of flowers beside it.
And a nightlight, a book.

> —"Stars"

But on the whole the poems of this new poet (who has moved from Plainfield) *move*. Partly because they have not after all entirely surrendered *angst*. Regardless of its various ripenings, *The Seven Ages* concludes with what I take to be a repudiation of the notion of a peace that passeth understanding and a renewed commitment to process:

Then I looked down and saw
the world I was entering, that would be my home.
And I turned to my companion, and I said *Where are we?*
And he replied *Nirvana.*
And I said again *But the light will give us no peace.*

> —"Fable"

For the moment, at least, the poet, not her guide, gets the last word, which of course her penultimate word has preempted. What has remained consistent is her struggle, her refusal of closure.

JOANNE FEIT DIEHL

An Interview with Louise Glück

The problem of the interview form is that candor looks like
grandiosity and demurral looks like idiocy. My discomfort in
this form (which is a problem of tone) is often mistaken for
unsociability or an intense need for privacy. Frankly, it seems
no one with a taste for privacy could possibly write: art is
too revealing. I don't mean because it is necessarily literally
autobiographical. I mean that, in its choice of metaphors, its
recurring concerns, it makes a highly specific portrait of an
individual mind.

The problem of the written word (and its magnetism) is
that it stays relatively fixed. This is harder to deal with in an
interview (which makes no aesthetic claims) than in a poem.
I may feel about these questions completely different in a
year's time, but the interview will fail to mirror that flux. And,
unfortunately, it seems more real in some ways than a poem
precisely because it is artless.

In any case, I change my mind, and my preferences, often.
These responses are current responses, as accurate and candid
as I can make them.

—L. G.

JOANNE FEIT DEIHL: Your earlier work has been perceived as both
grim and austere. How would you account for the shift from this
frame of mind to being more of a comic poet?

LOUISE GLÜCK: I don't know how to respond, since "grim" and
"austere" were never my words, never exactly the way I saw what I
was doing. "Austere" comes closer, though the word carries a kind
of puritanical suspiciousness, not simply of the voluptuous or
chaotic but of the inchoate, the mysterious. It *is* true that I wanted
to believe everything on the page was essential, a word I saw in
terms of what had been pared away (ornament, décor, what in film
we call special effects). As a reader, I had never been moved by pretty
tunes, lovely images. I wanted essence and spell, ideals that are, I

recognize, markedly static. What I loved, as a reader, haunted me not piecemeal but whole (though the poems were not always short).

In any case, I can understand the choice of that word, though it is not exactly my view. "Grim" doesn't correspond to any way in which I viewed my earlier (or present) work. Unless it is grim to write a poetry that does not soothe or placate or encourage (except in the sense that it might, if it worked, dignify a certain kind of struggle). Or grim to write without a taste for noble thought or moral heroism. Perception seems to me in its very essence not grim: it tacitly believes meaning exists, that experience has complexity and weight, that accuracy is of the most immense importance. Finally, I don't think of "grim" (which my dictionary calls rigid, stern, unrelenting, forbidding) to be a word of any spiritual dimension. And it seems to me spiritual hunger has driven my work from the beginning.

What is true, though, is that I had, earlier, a more pronounced taste for the elemental: meaning as opposed to meanings. That a certain oversimplification of experience may have been occurring (may still be occurring). I hope this isn't so, but my views on this subject would, obviously, bear the same taint as the poems bear—I'm not equipped to judge.

Pragmatically, at a certain point (around the time I began *Ararat*) I began to see that my work had rather stringently limited its tonal palate; it never, for example, sounded like my speech. This fact seemed to me curious and potentially fertile, not because the way I talked was better than the way I wrote, but because there might be interesting discoveries around the attempt to enlarge an existing range. I didn't, as I aged, develop a taste for comedy. Rather, I figured out how comic elements could be introduced; I began to learn, in *Ararat,* how to sound on the page the way I spoke. I liked the result; I felt, again, like an explorer. And my ambition for myself came to be an ambition to sustain, in a given work, an increasingly varied range of tones. "Given work" meant, at first, book; it came to mean poem. These days I try to make a poem swerve, to move unexpectedly from the luminous to the comic or ironic to the ecstatic, with each turn completely convincing, completely full. The old figure of keeping balls aloft seems exact to this attempt.

JFD: Your poems have consistently testified to an aesthetics based upon renunciation, a quest for perfection, and abstinence. In "Dedication to Hunger" *Descending Figure,* you write:

I felt
what I feel now aligning these words—
it is the same need to perfect,
of which death is the mere byproduct.

Yet, in the face of this self-imposed deprivation, you have continued over the years to sustain your creativity, writing increasingly powerful poems. How do you understand the relationship between this stance of deprivation and the psychic nurturance necessary to produce art?

LG: I do not believe psychic nurturance is necessary to the production of art. Arguably, artists as a group have had insufficient or claustrophobic experiences of nurture, for which art compensates them. Even belief in the self isn't absolutely necessary (though it is probably sporadically necessary). But sporadic belief can very easily coexist with, or alternate with, lacerating self-doubt.

This sounds very bleak. In fact I think it is a piece of amazing good fortune to have anything like a vocation for, or intense interest in, the making of art. The sustained blessing of my life has been the weird conviction that certain kinds of distilled utterance have unique, timeless, unquestioned value. This conviction confers meaning on experience. Even when I'm not capable of actually writing (which is often) I continue to feel, toward art, an extreme of reverence and awe. The point is this awe has nothing whatever to do with what I make, and everything to do with the form itself. I can't imagine trying to write without such reverence. But that, as far as I can tell, is the only essential.

I think, too, an underlying problem in the ideal of nurturance is that it tends to affirm what one is. Not only does this ignore the fact that art begins and survives as a craving, a hunger for what eludes, a beacon, a lighthouse, but it also contrives, by affirming the extant self, to paralyze. If the self is already worthy or lovable, how dare to change it? To expose in it something as yet unseen, something not incorporated into the existing affirmation?

The artist views that thing he might make, or dreams of making, as better than the self (though contaminated by, built out of the self). Contentment in being (of the kind that postulates the existing self as a kind of apotheosis) is, to me, a kind of dread. That and more is what the artist wants, I believe. All of us who are trying, somehow, to make something durable are driven by longing, and helped along by whatever allows the belief that the thing that eludes will one day no longer elude. But such people would continue to try, helplessly, even in the absence of belief. It may be that the difficulty of the task, the artist's periodic or extended inability, finally fortifies conviction, lends it stature.

JFD: How do you spend your days?

LG: How I spend days depends partly on external facts: whether or not I'm teaching (which means, for me, commuting, living in two places), whether or not I'm doing frequent readings. The deepest variables occur, however, in less practical areas; my life varies most dramatically around the issue of writing. And I write, the last decade or so, in an increasingly bizarre way, either in a sustained furious blitz or not at all. These rhythms are completely independent of the issues around earning a living: they have nothing to do with available time or available solitude. When I'm writing, I write anywhere: hotel rooms, airplanes, exercise classes, elevators, grocery stores, in the blank pages of class texts. I can also, ample evidence proves, not write anywhere: the bucolic serene, the pure uninterrupted privacy of the empty room do not reliably help me. They tend, in fact, to do the reverse: any attempt to make a ceremony of the fact of writing, to prepare for it, to create, in the house, that shrine at which the work is done—such attempts have, generally, completely silenced me. They are, for me, far more taxing, far more frightening, than the demands and pressures of the classroom, the obligations and structure of daily life.

This fact seems to me quite liberating: in the one area most crucial to me, the area of writing, I need not make my life perfect—to do so only makes the art less likely. Liberating and an immense relief: I am simply in the hands of something, some periodic hunger. My need to make perfect (which exhausts me and has driven many around me crazy) can spend itself on other agendas, like cooking, bouquet making, lifting weights.

When I'm writing (which occurs every two to three years, roughly, though some of the recent books, like *Meadowlands,* were written in my earlier tortoise manner combined with the sort of intensity I've described) I sleep less; I wake up every hour or half hour; I make a few notes in the dark. Usually I go back to sleep immediately; sometimes I wake again ten minutes later, and ten minutes after that. Sometimes I simply stay awake, because the ideas are too rapid, or because I'm afraid I won't be able to read my writing in the morning. This is the only time I allow myself proximity to tools: paper, pen. Other times, to make the tools available seems to me a jinx, like the attempt to build the special room with the special view, all in order to compose. When I'm writing, my general state could be described as focused obliviousness; I become quite dramatically accident prone (more than usual). When I'm not writing, my general state is a sort of diffuse anxiety. The cusp, the going from writing to not writing, often produces enormous tension. The first time this occurred really dramatically was after the writing of *The Wild Iris,* most of which was done in a single summer. My then husband (very shrewdly) remarked, when the book was done, that I was going to be really hungover. That was his word. I told him nothing of the sort would occur, thinking (mistakenly) that I had attained a fluent mastery and euphoric serenity that would never falter. In fact, I developed that autumn a series of pronounced facial tics and twitches, augmenting an unusually exhausting round of intense somatizing—terror, darkness, a sort of favorite hits of lethal diseases.

I now expect this sort of thing; it seems reasonable that such concentrated endeavor (whether it feels, as sometimes, like exaltation and at other times simply the happiness of being able to work steadily—a much more modest and theoretically less taxing state) should produce in its wake some kind of unraveling. And I am grateful to the fact that I have obligations in the world, to my friends, to my students: they help in the negotiation of transitions. This sounds, I know, like mania, but it doesn't altogether match descriptions I've read or heard in that the feeling of wild possession (and sometimes mastery) is highly specific to a single task, like an athlete's training. The writing wasn't only nocturnal: it went on during the day, too, in odd gusts alternating with routine activity, like folding laundry. Nights I was torn, after awhile, between desperately wanting sleep and wanting another poem.

What doesn't vary, whether I'm writing or not, whether I'm traveling or not, is my need, in every area but writing, for ritual and structure. I can ritualize almost anything; travel is hard for me, obviously, because it cannot be ritualized. I develop, in the various lives I lead, certain organizing tasks and pleasures. The exercise studio, the gym, the public library, the market. And so on.

Finally this: the older I get, the more acute my pleasure in ordinary life. Fitful, certainly, but acute. My yearning toward perfection, an ideal of receptivity as much as anything else, has been, periodically,

less punishing; in its place, a somewhat greater capacity for contentment and gratitude. Daily life seems to me a miracle: at times, when
I feel this less vividly, I feel some of the frenzied unhappiness that
used to attach to the idea of perfection. I never expected, frankly, to
last this long. Nor did I have, when I was young, any willingness to
be pleased by the partial; I thought to be pleased by it would be
to be condemned to it; I thought the ordinary was merely prepara-
tion. All this, the pleasure of daily life, seems worth remarking because
my capacity to suffer, or generate suffering, seems more obvious.

JFD: What do you regret not having accomplished so far?

LG: Regret is not something I suffer from. Or feel. The same holds
true for its corollary, nostalgia. This is not to suggest that I am free of
a certain kind of psychological ordeal. But for me, the ordeal is always imminent, or in the moment. If I am not prone to regret, I am
most vividly and chronically prone to anxiety; not sorrow over the
thing missed, but terror lest the future be missed or contaminated.

I very rarely think of my past work. Except insofar as I read from
older work, from time to time, at readings. But it always seems to
me not mine. Sometimes it will strike me as too good to be mine,
its virtues a reprimand to the self I have become. More often, I'll
be humiliated by its limitations. But shame, appalled disgust at the
self's limitations, is not the same as regretted action or regretted
failure to act. And much of my anxiety reflects a relentless need to
either (depending on my mood) correct or equal the art of the self
I once was. My anxiety in regard to the uncertain, the future (as
opposed to the past), has uncountable forms. If I'm writing well, I
feel terror lest I not be permitted to finish (the poem, the book). If
I have written well, and finished something I feel pride in, I worry
that I'll have to pay for it somehow. Then I worry that I won't be
able, ever again, to work at that level. That fear, even immediately
after the finishing of a book, in the period when I ought to be
proud for about seven minutes, demonstrates the degree to which
the completed thing (in my work, and, often, in my emotional life)
has retreated: it is either not mine, or mine but worthless. The past
is, in my lexicon, as absolute, potent, sometimes, as judgment. The
limitations that obsess me are the limitations of the possible, which
lie in the future.

I believe, somehow (possibly foolishly), in a certain spiritual cor-
rectness to these struggles, as I believe in ordeal. And yet I've won-
dered lately about this belief, which seems to fetishize a propensity

for suffering that may be serving other, more damaging purposes. I should also add that I tend to believe in ordeal most vigorously when I am not undergoing it, which is to say, when I've written something, or been relieved of any physical problem. At these moments I believe it is the form of a soul's negotiation with chance, an attempt to wrest profit from what cannot be changed.

Berryman has wonderful lines on these themes in his essay on Anne Frank: "We have been tracing a psychological and moral development to which, if I am right, no close parallel can be found. It took place under very special circumstances, which—let us now conclude as she concluded—though superficially unfavorable, in fact highly favorable to it; she was *forced* to mature, in order to survive; the hardest challenge, let's say, that a person can face without defeat is the best for him. And anyway, we are all defeated; Hemingway once put it that the only point is to make the enemy pay as heavily as possible for *your* position; this she certainly did."

That both Berryman and Hemingway were suicides does not compromise the power of these perceptions; it merely affirms that they knew this subject, having been forced, like Anne Frank, though in different ways, to live at its heart. About which neither had any choice.

A coda: what I understand about regret I understand because of greed. I regret, for example, that (because I want to remain relatively lean) I don't have all the ice cream I want, that I turn away from certain recipes, that I experience, rarely, the barbaric ecstasies of red meat. In my life as a writer, nothing corresponds quite to this keen sense of the moment missed, a regret that the mechanism of control is so honed. And I understand loss; I have I suppose a vocation for mourning. But this seems to me not regret, but rather an experience, like anxiety, of helplessness.

LOUISE GLÜCK

Afterword

The Restorative Power of Art

This subject seems to me two subjects: the experience of the writer and the experience of the reader.

The title of this panel corresponds, I think, solely to the experience of the reader, for whom a work of art can make a kind of mantra: by giving form to devastation, the poem rescues the reader from a darkness without shape or gravity; it is an island in a free fall; it becomes his companion in grief, his rescuer, a proof that suffering can be made somehow to yield meaning.

But the relation of the poet to his composition seems to me other.

We live in a culture almost fascistic in its enforcement of optimism. Great shame attaches to the idea and spectacle of ordeal: the incentive to suppress or deny or truncate ordeal is manifested in two extremes—the cult of perfect health (both physical and psychological) and, at the other end, what could be called a pornography of scars, the seemingly endless flood of memoirs and poems and novels rooted in the assumption that the exhibition of suffering must make authentic and potent art. But if suffering is so hard, why should its expression be easy? Trauma and loss are not, in themselves, art: they are like half a metaphor. In fact, the kind of work I mean—however true its personal source—is tainted by a kind of preemptive avidity. It seems too ready to inhabit the most dramatic extremes; too ready to deny loss as continuity, as immutable fact. It proposes instead a narrative of personal triumph, a narrative filled with markers like "growth" and "healing" and "self-realization" and culminating in the soul's unqualified or comprehensive declaration of wholeness, as though loss were merely a catalyst for self-improvement. But as the power of loss is undermined or denied, so too does the speaker come to seem entirely constructed, inhuman.

Presented at a symposium at the Boston Institute for Psychotherapy.

My own experience of acute suffering, whether in the life or in the work, is that during such periods I do pretty much nothing but try to stay alive, the premise being that if I stay alive I will at least be present in case something changes. I have no sense of myself as trying to effect change. Nor do I believe that the peculiar resilience of the artist is a function of art's restorative power. The artist's experience of his own work alternates panic with gratitude. What is constant, what seems to me the source of resilience (or fortitude), is a capacity for intense, driven absorption. Such absorption makes a kind of intermission from the self; it derives, in the artist, from a deep belief in the importance of art (though not necessarily his own art, except in the presence of its being made). At intervals throughout his life, the artist is taken out of that life by concentration; he lives for a time in a suspension that is also a quest, a respite that is also acute tension. His belief in art, and investment in art, in the dream of articulation, project him constantly into the future—the hypothetical moment in which comprehensive darkness acquires limits and form. For nostalgia, it substitutes terror and hunger; for the ideal of restoration it substitutes an ideal of discovery. Toward which end, the artist, like the analyst, cultivates a disciplined refusal of self-deception, which is less a moral position than a pragmatic act, since the only possible advantage of suffering is that it may afford insight.

The great crime writer Ross Macdonald has observed that he "like many writers" "couldn't work directly with [his] own experiences or feelings." For Macdonald, a narrator "had to be interposed, like protective lead, between [himself], and the radioactive material." For the poet, time suffices, in that it introduces an altered perspective. But those works of art that can be traced directly to specific events—however long after the fact they may be created—involve the artist in a particular relation to those events. The poem is a revenge on loss, which has been forced to yield to a new form, a thing that hadn't existed in the world before. The loss itself becomes, then, both addition and subtraction: without it, there would not have been this poem, this novel, this work in stone. And a strange sense of betrayal of the past can occur as the absolute of loss becomes ambiguous, the mutilator the benefactor. Such complex doubling of function doesn't seem to me a thing restored. And the agent of transformation, in any case, is time, which cannot be forced or rushed.

Contributors

Frank Bidart has published five books of poems, the most recent, *Music Like Dirt* (2002). With David Gewanter, Bidart edited *Robert Lowell's Collected Poems* (2003). *Star Dust,* his new volume of poetry, will be published in May 2005. Bidart lives in Cambridge, Massachusetts, and teaches at Wellesley College.

Paul Breslin, a professor at Northwestern University, teaches and researches modern and contemporary American poetry and West Indian literature. He is the author of *The Psycho-Political Muse: American Poetry Since the Fifties* (1987); *You Are Here* (poems, fall 2000); and *Nobody's Nation: Reading Derek Walcott* (2001). A second book of poems is nearing completion. With Robert Hamner, he has coedited a special Derek Walcott issue of *Callaloo,* which appeared in winter 2005.

Stephen Burt teaches poetry, poetry writing, and twentieth-century literature at Macalester College in St. Paul, Minnesota. His books include *Randall Jarrell and His Age* and *Popular Music,* a collection of poems; he is currently editing *Randall Jarrell on W. H. Auden* (forthcoming) and completing a second book of poems.

Bonnie Costello is professor of English at Boston University. Her most recent book is *Shifting Ground: Reinventing Landscape in Modern American Poetry.* She is currently working on *Planets on Tables,* a study of still life motifs in art and literature from 1930 to 1950.

Joanne Feit Diehl, a professor at the University of California, Davis, is the author of *Dickinson and the Romantic Imagination* (1981); *Women Poets and the American Sublime* (1990); and *Elizabeth Bishop and Marianne Moore: The Psychodynamics of Creativity* (1993). She is currently at work on a project that investigates the interactions of psychoanalysis and art.

Sandra M. Gilbert, a professor of English at the University of California, Davis, has coauthored or coedited a number of books with

Susan Gubar of Indiana University; these include *The Madwoman in the Attic: The Woman Writer & the 19th-Century Literary Imagination; No Man's Land: The Place of the Woman Writer in the 20th Century* (in three volumes); and *The Norton Anthology of Literature by Women: The Traditions in English*. In addition she has published seven collections of her own poetry—most recently *Belongings*—as well as a memoir, *Wrongful Death*. Her latest critical work, *Death's Door: Modern Dying & the Ways We Grieve*, will be published in January 2006.

Linda Gregerson's most recent book of poems, *Waterborne*, was the winner of the Kingsley Tufts Poetry Award. Gregerson is also the author of *The Woman Who Died in Her Sleep* (1996), *Fire in the Conservatory* (1982), and two books of criticism, *Negative Capability: Contemporary American Poetry* (2001) and *The Reformation of the Subject: Spenser, Milton, and the English Protestant Epic* (1995). She is professor of English at the University of Michigan.

Wayne Koestenbaum has published three books of poetry, most recently *The Milk of Inquiry*, and five books of prose, most recently *Andy Warhol*. He is a professor of English at the Graduate Center of the City University of New York.

James Longenbach is the author of two books of poems, *Fleet River* and *Threshold*, as well as several books of literary criticism, most recently *The Resistance to Poetry* and *Modern Poetry after Modernism*. He is Joseph H. Gilmore Professor of English at the University of Rochester.

Alan Williamson is professor of English at the University of California, Davis. He is the author of four books of poetry and four of criticism, most recently *Almost a Girl: Male Writers and Female Identification*.

Stephen Yenser's book of poems *The Fire in All Things* won the Walt Whitman Award from the Academy of American Poets. The author of *A Boundless Field: American Poetry at Large, The Consuming Myth: The Work of James Merrill*, and *Circle to Circle: The Poetry of Robert Lowell*, and coeditor (with J. D. McClatchy) of the *Collected Poems* of James Merrill, he is professor of English and Director of Creative Writing at UCLA.